Horace Bushnell

Women's Suffrage

The Reform Against Nature

Horace Bushnell

Women's Suffrage
The Reform Against Nature

ISBN/EAN: 9783742809360

Manufactured in Europe, USA, Canada, Australia, Japa

Cover: Foto ©ninafisch / pixelio.de

Manufactured and distributed by brebook publishing software (www.brebook.com)

Horace Bushnell

Women's Suffrage

WOMEN'S SUFFRAGE;

THE

REFORM AGAINST NATURE.

BY

HORACE BUSHNELL.

———————

NEW YORK:
CHARLES SCRIBNER AND COMPANY.
1869.

Entered according to Act of Congress, in the year 1869,
By CHARLES SCRIBNER & Co.,
In the Clerk's Office of the District Court of the United States for
the Southern District of New York.

TO THE PUBLIC.

It is not to be supposed that this little volume has finished the argument of a subject so large, and, in former times, so entirely unattempted. If it brings the question to some fixed issue, taking it away from the mere chance-working it has had hitherto, it will have done the service proposed. And if the projected reform is totally different from all other reforms, in the times gone by, in the fact that it is a reform against nature—an attempt to make trumpets out of flutes, and sun-flowers out of violets, the discovery can not be difficult, and it will save us much trouble if it is made soon.

I take pleasure in acknowledging my obligations to Rev. Mr. Alger, in his book on the Friendships of Women, for a good many historic facts and references that would otherwise have cost me much labor. Also, to Rev. George B. Bacon, of Orange, New Jersey, for the history of Women's Suffrage in that State.

I do not propose to continue this discussion, but to abide the criticisms laid upon me with what of patience I am able.

ACKNOWLEDGMENT.

For once I will dare to break open one of the customary seals of silence, by inscribing this little book to the woman I know best and most thoroughly; having been overlapped, as it were, and curtained in the same consciousness for the last thirty-six years. If she is offended that I do it without her consent, I hope she may get over the offense shortly, as she has a great many others that were worse. She has been with me in many weaknesses and some storms, giving strength alike in both; sharp enough to see my faults, faithful enough to expose them, and considerate enough to do it wisely; shrinking never from loss, or blame, or shame to be encountered in any thing right to be done; adding great and high instigations—instigations always to good, and never to evil mistaken for good; forecasting always things bravest and best to be done, and supplying inspirations enough to have made a hero, if they had not lacked the timber. If I have done any thing well, she has been the more really in it that she did not know it, and the more willingly also that having her part in it known has not even occurred to her; compelling me thus to honor not less, but more, the covert glory of the womanly nature; even as I obtain a distincter, and more wondering apprehension of the divine meanings, and moistenings, and countless, unbought ministries, it contributes to this otherwise very dry world.

H. B.

CONTENTS.

I.
PRELIMINARY—QUESTION STATED, ...   Page 9

II.
NO RIGHT OF SUFFRAGE ABSOLUTE IN MAN OR WOMAN,   32

III.
WOMEN NOT CREATED OR CALLED TO GOVERN, ...   49

IV.
SCRIPTURE DOCTRINE COINCIDES, ...   73

V.
SUBTLE MISTAKES OF FEELING AND ARGUMENT, . . .   88

VI.
THE REPORT OF HISTORY, ...   110

VII.
PROBABLE EFFECTS, ...   134

VIII.
PROSPECTS AND POSSIBILITIES OF WOMEN.   164

WOMEN'S SUFFRAGE.

I.

PRELIMINARY.—QUESTION STATED.

If we do not know how it is, or why, we do at least know the fact, (that power somehow naturally runs to oppression.) We oppress the animals; we oppress the wild untutored species of our own race; rulers take it for long ages as their divine right to oppress their subjects; even the church of God has been a mighty hunter of its people in the name of love; and in much the same manner it will be seen that the whole male half of the race, having power to do it, have been piling weights of disability and depression on the female half. Probably it can not be said that man has undertaken purposely to be the oppressor of woman—he would scorn the impeachment; protesting, on the contrary, his natural admirations, his zeal to serve and protect, the profuseness of his attentions, and the unstinted tribute of respect and deference he is always wont to render. And yet, little as he means it, he is nevertheless gravitating steadily toward some practice of wrong against the sex; laying up usages that are oppressive, maxims unjust, laws of really despotic mastership; all, it would seem, because the wrong is in him and, having the power, must needs be somehow issued in the deed; even though he disavows it and protests he would not have it.

In this manner it results that the lot of woman comes to be a lot of abridgment and suppression, much more commonly than we have been observing ourselves. As our attention is called to the matter, and we become more completely awake to it, we are surprised to find how many disadvantages are laid upon the condition of woman that no principle of equity permits, and no pretense of reason or necessity justifies. It does not surprise us that, in the savage and barbarous forms of society, she is reduced to the lot of a menial or drudge and well nigh to a beast of burden; or that she is bought and sold for marriage, apart from any right of consent, and consigned in this manner to a husband whose power is a power of life and death. All such monstrous kinds of wrong we expect to encounter in the barbaric conditions of society. But the real wonder now forcing itself upon our discovery, is that our own deliberately adjusted laws and institutions are so often unequal, as regards the property rights of men and women and the redress of their personal wrongs; that women are so often excluded, whether by law or public usage, from modes of employment and productive industry that are equally appropriate or even more appropriate to them; that having thus only about one-third the number of employments that men have, they are penned, as it were, before that third, and create a competition that reduces their wages to the smallest pittance—penned of course for unrighteous prey, in whatever manner the terrible stringency of their lot, may be said in a sense to compel. Looking over this whole chapter of our civil and social state, we are mortified to find how largely it is a chapter of wrongs, or of only half vindicated rights. At one time we get angry, at another we can do nothing but take our doses of shame in silence. But the anger and the shame are both salutary; for they are stirring us up to a more and more determined purpose of redress. The true basis of relationship between the sexes, is going now to be thoroughly investigated, and we shall not rest again till it is cleared and established.

Of course there is nothing to be gained by any overstatement of the wrongs of woman, or by any demands that exceed the proportion of their powers and conditions. It is nothing that they can not get as high wages as men, when they can not do as much, or do it as well. It is nothing that they can not get the wages of rugged and dangerous employments, in such as are gentle and delicate. It is nothing that in great poverty, sin-

gle women or women having families are brought
into conditions of unspeakable severity ; the same
is true of men, and we do not expect them to sink
mournfully or moaningly under their lot, but to
bravely bear, and dig, and climb till they are free.
No better chance for poor women can ever be
asked; or if it is they will never get it; and it will
always be possible, both for poor discouraged men
to justify rushing into the very worst and vilest
trades to get their bread, and for poor discouraged
women to justify their imbrutement in a specially
disgusting livelihood permitted by their sex. The
only way, in all such unfavoring conditions and
straits of peril, both for women and for men, and for
one as truly as for the other, is to suffer patiently
and fight bravely; and thank God women are at
least equal in this kind of capacity. Again, it is
nothing that women, sewing women for example,
are not helped directly in the matter of their wages
by legal enactment, any more than that men are
not—there is no such possibility as a legally ap-
pointed rate of wages ; market price is the only
scale of earning possible for women as for men.
The only help that can be given them is a wider
range of employments, and personal additions of
character and capacity, that will put their services
in a higher rate of estimation. Education more
advanced will give a more advanced capacity, and
the educated eye and hand will do a better and
more valuable service. Besides, the rate of wages

depends in a considerable degree, on the amount of personality in the workers, and the estimate had of their quality. If women have sometimes been depressed by sex legislation, they will not have the damage repaired by any beneficiary sex legislation that gives them artificial and really forced advantages.

We have made a good and right beginning already in the matter of education, and the beneficent results that come along with our new codes of training are even a surprise to us; compelling us to rectify a great many foolish prejudices that we supposed to be sanctioned as inevitable wisdom, by long ages of experience. The joining, for example, of the two sexes in common studies and a common college life—what could be more un-university-like, and, morally speaking, more absurd！ And, as far as the young women are concerned, what could be more unwomanly and really more improper! I confess, with some mortification, that when the thing was first done, I was not a little shocked even by the rumor of it. But when, by and by, some fifteen years ago, I drifted into Oberlin and spent a Sunday there, I had a new chapter opened that has cost me the loss of a considerable cargo of wise opinions, all scattered in loose wreck never again to be gathered. I found that the old church idea of a college (*collegium*), where youths of the male sex were gathered to the cloisters of their male teachers, the monks, and where any sight and thought of a woman approaching the place was conceived to be a profanation, was itself a dismal imposture, and a kind of total lie against every thing most beneficent in the bisexual order of our existence. I learned, for the first time, what it means that the sexes, not merely as by two-and-two, but as a large open scale of society, have a complementary relation, existing as helps to each other, and that humanity is a disjointed creature running only to waste and disorder, where they are put so far asunder as to leave either one or the other, in a properly monastic and separate state. Here were gathered for instruction large numbers of pupils, male and female, pursuing their studies together in the same classes and lessons, under the same teachers; the young women deriving a more pronounced and more positive character in their mental training from association with young men in their studies, and the young men a closer and more receptive refinement and a more delicate habitual respect to what is in personal life, from their associations with young women. The discipline of the institution, watchful as it properly should be, was yet a kind of silence, and was practically null — being carried on virtually by the mutually qualifying and restraining powers of the sexes over each other. There was scarcely a single case of discipline, or almost never more than one, occurring in a year.

In particular there was no such thing known as an *esprit du corps* in deeds of mischief, no conspiracies against order and the faculty, no bold prominence in evil aspired to, no lying proudly done for the safety of the clan, no barbarities of hazing perpetrated. And so the ancient, traditional, hell-state of college life, and all the immense ruin of character propagated by the club-law of a stringently male or monastic association, was totally escaped and put away. What we see occurring always, where males are gathered in a society by themselves, whether in the prison, or the shop, or the school, or the army—every beginning of the *esprit du corps* in evil is kept under, shamed away, made impossible by the association of the gentler sex, who can not co-operate in it, and can not think of it with respect.

And what so long ago was proved by this earliest experiment, has since been proved a dozen or twenty times over by other experiments under other forms of religion, as well as under all varieties of literary culture and social atmosphere. Thus if any one should imagine that the success of this first trial at Oberlin was due to the particular, very strongly pronounced type of religious influence there established, he may hear President Mann, of the Unitarian College at Antioch, where also the two sexes were combined in the same studies, uniting in the testimony—" We have the most orderly, sober, diligent, exemplary institution in the country. We passed through the last term and are more than half through the present; and I have not had occasion to make a single entry of any misdemeanor in our record book—not a case for any serious discipline. There is no rowdyism in the village, no nocturnal rampages making night hideous. All is quiet, peaceful; and the women of the village feel the presence of our students, when met in the streets in the evening, to be a protection rather than an exposure. It is almost five years since I came here, and, as yet, I have had no practical joke or college prank, as they are called, played upon me—not in a single instance." A very intelligent writer in the *Westminster Review*, acquainted with this and with many other colleges, testifies to the decisive superiority here in moral behavior, and puts double honor on the name before so transcendently honored, by saying, in a touch of pleasantry, that "male students were first called gentlemen at Antioch."

The experiment of joining the two sexes in the same studies, and composing in that manner the society of college life, has now been carried far enough, I think, to show that it is the only plan which is really according to nature. Whether the colleges and universities of the old monastic type will change in their organizations, so as to claim their advantages in the better way discovered, remains to be seen. Perhaps they would not do it if they could, and perhaps they can not do it if they would. It remains, in either case, to be seen whether they have benefits of any kind, sufficient to compensate for their moral disadvantages, and so to keep them still in existence.

The two sexes brought together in this manner, it is hardly necessary to say, will be rapidly discovering their true scale of merit. It matters little whether they are found to be equal or unequal in their talent of scholarship; for it does not follow that the greatest facility of acquirement will be issued in the greatest power, or will even be felt as having now the greatest practical breadth and volume. Enough, that both sexes will better understand, and more respect each other, and will learn to take their relative places more exactly and gracefully. That they have in fact a complementary nature one to the other, will be distinctly felt, and all but visibly seen; and the college itself, in its double combination of male and female impulse, will be only a more complete man or humanity, than it otherwise could be. The male talent, and the female, will be a great deal more exactly apprehended than they have been. It will even be seen that sex is predicable of talent as of organization, and both sexes of mind will be receiving qualities and contributions from each other in their cross relations, such as answer with general exactness to the husbanding and meet helping of the marriage bond itself.

Educated on this footing of equality, women will very soon escape their unrighteous disabilities, and obtain a place in the scale of estimation that exactly corresponds with their personal weight and capacity, and more than that they have no right to ask. Employments will be open to them just according to what they are best qualified to do, and their wages, like the wages also of men, will be in the exact compound ratio of what they can do, and what they personally are. And as what they personally are includes a great deal of favor to their woman's look and voice, they will scarcely miss the full reward of their industry.

As they have been educated with men, they will also become educators with men, and if they can fill the highest, most responsible places of management and presiding trust, they must and will obtain such places, and the rewards that men have in the same. They will have professorships allowed them, such as they can more appropriately fill —not of mechanical philosophy perhaps, or chemistry, or metallurgy, or fortification, but of the languages, of botany, of moral science, and, not improperly, of the exact mathematics.

Meantime, the different learned professions will be opened a certain way, at least, in offers of engagement, as the profession of medicine is doing now. The practice of medicine is, to a great extent, proper to women as to men, and is often a great deal more proper to women. In cases of surgery, the steady and firm hand of a man is indispensable. At the same time, a great many cases occur where, over and above the necessary proprieties of sex, a practice is wanted that combines both nursing and medicine, and for all such cases a female physician is even required. That we have educated female physicians already in the field, engaged in a large and lucrative practice is, in this view, a matter of fair congratulation. It will do no harm, but will properly gladden a great many friends of humanity, if their number is largely increased.

Our women are less forward in claiming a place in the legal profession, though, in one or two cases a preparation for it is reported as now begun. Perhaps it may some time be discovered that the proper work of this profession is capable of being divided, or set in two departments, one of which is altogether suitable for women. First, there is a silent, in-door, office work, that includes the investigation of authorities and the citation of precedents; the framing of legal documents, such as deeds, contracts, pleadings, and the like; the notary-public functions; and, why not often? the clerkships of courts of record. In the second will be classed the out-door hunt of crimes, frauds, and disguised ownerships; the uncovering and preparing of evidences; the advocacies and public litigations of causes. This second department is only for men; for, whatever we may think of their talents, women are quite out of place in this kind of engagement. No doubt they often have the talent necessary to maintain, or manage a cause. The wonderful adroitness and persistency and more than lawyer-like resource, or insight of law, displayed by Mrs. Gaines in the conduct of her suit, are sufficient evidence of this. But the battle she maintained was to vindicate her own right, not that of another; and perhaps she was saved, by this fact, from some of the very disagreeable personal effects that would otherwise have followed. Still, we have good right to say that, if we will have women left us and not mere female men, there is no woman who can pitch herself into the wrangle, and debate, and vehement fight of a bar, and do it for a living, without becoming a virago shortly. Her eye, her look, her voice, her impetuous action will suggest a knife-blade edge sooner than some would think. The soft lines will vanish; the music that was will be sharpened to clangor, the bold air will dismiss the modesty, and the general expression will be—"caution! have a caution!" Saying nothing of the change which has cost us a woman, the unmaking she suffers in her voice and manners, will reduce her shortly, without fail, to a very unpopular, ineffective advocate. And it would be even a greater mistake for her to think of being a more qualified judge, because of the finer equity of her womanly dispositions. Indeed it is a considerable part of her incapacity that she is not wicked enough to sift, expose, and vigorously score the lying tricks of evidence. Besides, women lack authority, and never bear it well when they assume it. A judge who has nerve to support the even poise of authority during all the intricacies of a whole week's trial, must be more than a remarkable woman therefore—a kind of Radamanthus, somewhat manlier than a man.

But if women are allowed to find a sphere open, in the office-work side of the legal profession, it will be a very great advantage gained for them as regards the range of their employment, even though they should consent to have no part in the litigant operations of courts and causes. It would give them also a more prominent and distinctly admitted place in the world of business.

Precisely what is allowable, or not allowable, to women, as regards the clerical profession, it may not be easy to determine; only it is clear as need be that a much larger and more forward operation is permissible, without damage to the Christian order, and with real advantage to the Christian cause. We have many more Christian women than Christian men; their piety ranges higher, and they have many of them higher gifts of experience, and practically speaking, a more instructed insight of the Christian truth and life.

They pray more and commonly know better how to pray. They do more volunteer work. So richly gifted, have we still no use to make of them, better than to put an extinguisher on them and keep them in suppression? If we think we are detained by Scripture usage and law, we can at least fulfill the Scripture usage, and make deaconesses of them. And if we can make three or four of them deaconesses, we can, with as little disorder, make a much greater number if we please, and set them forth on missions of public service; as Phebe the deaconess of the church at Cenchrea was sent, in that manner, to Rome. And if they used their office well, would they not " purchase to themselves a good degree and great boldness in the faith," even as the deacons might in theirs? A single glance in this direction shows that a large field is here open to the ministrations of Christian women, a much larger field than, as yet, they have been called to occupy.

As regards the ministry of the word, or the matter of public speaking in the churches, it is very evident that what Paul lays down as restriction in the 11th and 14th chapters of his First Epistle to the Corinthians—requiring in the former that no woman pray or prophesy with her head uncovered, and in the latter that she keep silence altogether—that all such restriction is now gone by, in the going by of the particular specified reasons in which it was based; viz.: the public " shame " or scandal it would be to religion, under the then accepted laws of womanly modesty, and the current impressions of disgrace incurred and decency violated, when these laws are disregarded. "Shame," and again "shame," is the consideration on which he turns his argument for restriction, first in one case and then in the other. But we of the present age have no longer any feeling that a woman throws off her modesty because she speaks unveiled; though, in Turkey and some other parts of the world, that feeling may still prevail. We have still our likes and dislikes, in one degree or another, to the public speaking of women in all sorts of assemblies; but almost nobody imagines that a woman who simply prays in the Spirit, or takes what Jeremy Taylor calls "the liberty of prophesying," in public meetings for religion, is therefore broken loose from the proper restraints of delicacy. It is our general conviction that scenes of battle and high wrestling are not for women, and that when they go in to wrangle thus with men, they had much better be somewhere else; but nobody has ever observed that Lucretia Mott, or any speaker of the Quaker sisterhood, long practiced in the prophesying of the Spirit, has been hardening in voice, or look, or becoming in any respect less womanly. So far the restrictions of the "shame" are gone by, and the right of speaking for religion, under the inspirations of religion, belongs apparently to women as to men

And if women have gifts that qualify them specially for such ministrations, there appears to be no good reason longer why they should be kept under the ban of silence.

But the question of ministration is one thing, and the question of administration another. And it is to cut off this, as I understand, that the apostle has enjoined it on women to "keep silence in the churches; for it is not permitted them," he says, " to speak, but to be under obedience, as also saith the law." The "speaking" here intended, appears to be not exactly prophesying and praying in the Spirit, for these he appears to have just now allowed, under the restriction of a veil; but a speaking as in council and authority—a debating of administrative matters, where they will put themselves in measure with men, and assume a power of leadership which does not belong to them—is plainly meant to be included. When, accordingly, we ask how far the clerical profession is open, or may be, to women, there is no objection to allowing that anything which belongs to the quickening, and edifying of assemblies in the Spirit may be left open to them; only when we come to matters of church administration and presiding rule, these do not come within their jurisdiction. They can not, in true Christian order, be made pastors, or presbyters, or bishops; no one of the apostles ever heard of such a thing. What a catalogue of honorable women does the apostle recite, in the last chapter of his Epistle to the Romans:—Phebe, "succorer of many," including also the apostle himself; Priscilla, named before her husband, as having "periled even her own neck," with his, for the apostle's deliverance, "to whom all the churches of the Gentiles now give thanks;" "Mary, who bestowed much labor" on the apostle himself; Junia, named with respect, as having been "in Christ before him," and as being now a character "of note among the apostles;" "Persis who labored much in the Lord;" Rufus' mother whom the great apostle loves to salute in the title "his mother and mine." What homage and respect does he testify to these heroic women, and what estimate does he hold of their almost common ministry with him, in the word and sacrifice of Jesus! He had work enough for them, such as many of our fastidious over-orderly patrons of order are never finding any place to allow; and yet the nearest he ever came to putting any one of them in rule, was when he allowed a single one of them as a deaconess in her little suburban chapel. Our conclusion is, on the whole, that, as in the medical and legal professions, so in the clerical, there is a large department of ministry and service that may properly be open to women, though no official right of administration or presiding rule is permitted. It is even conceivable that a considerable number of women, fitly trained, should carry on the quickening and edifying work in as many churches, under the presiding oversight and rule of some common presbyter or bishop, doing every one of them, it may be, a greater and more valued work than he.

How far we may rightfully and hopefully go in setting open to women a wider range of employments, and by that means increasing the rate of wages for their labor, will here be seen. I might dwell, in the same manner, on the advantage they will gain and have already gained, by assuming their place in the field of art and literary production. What better, higher names can we ask in this field than Mrs. Stowe, Margaret Fuller, Gail Hamilton, and the long and brilliant train that follow in the inspiration of their example, and the courage raised by their success. All such victories gotten by the sex are gotten for the whole sex, and even for the humblest and most undistinguished members. They are raised universally in personal consideration, and more employments at higher wages are open to them. And then, the more things they do and do well, the more they will be called to do. They will take the field of common school education largely to themselves, and their compensations will be graduated by their service. They will get hold of the ideas and laws of business, and their business faculty will be more respected. And so they will take a more forward part in the trades; sometimes on their own account, and sometimes in the subordinate ranges of clerkship, book-keeping, and the like. They will thus begin, ere long, to conquer places and ranges of business from which formerly they were excluded, becoming, not improperly, managers of hotels, bank-tellers, brokers, actuaries of insurances, private bankers, type-setters, overseers of printing. Breaking into such new fields, they will cease to crowd each other as now, by an over-supply in the market of operative industry; till finally the poor sewing women will obtain some easement of their truly hard lot—the grace of mitigation will be reaching down even to them. They will no more work and die as now, but they will begin to work and live. I do not say or think that women will ever obtain, in the general, as high wages as men, partly because the number of their employments must be much smaller, and partly because they can not always do an equal, or equally perfect style of work.

The great departments of agriculture, engineering, and war, seafaring, railroad, making, architecture, machine building, all the heaviest, roughest, tensest forms of creative labor are reserved for men. Almost any woman would even think it an affront to be offered a part in them. Indeed, she has neither muscle, nor eye, nor hand, for these engagements. How often do we hear it asserted as a fact unquestionable and well understood, that no sewing woman was ever yet able to make a perfect, gentleman's, coat. Sewing all her life long, she has never obtained the precision of eye, and firm guidance of hand necessary to this very nicely combined, delicately complex, really constructive whole of stitch-work. And it is only just that men should have this advantage; for if they could not excel in the mechanical perfectness and precision of all such mechanical labor, they would sink to a dishonored grade, as being only the world's male drudges, in bearing, as they must, all the roughest offices, and hardest, coarsest forms of service. And if women are disposed to complain that they can not do as perfect work as men, let them take their compensation in the fact that they are excused everywhere, except among savages, from the hardest, and most nearly animal drudgeries of labor. And if their works require no such tension of faculty as may set the exactness of their hand, and the firm precision of their motions, it must be sufficient for them that a fine flexibility and grace of action are left them, to be their special ornament.

It will be understood, of course, in our contrivances of ways to enlarge the spheres and advance the opportunities of women, that they are to be carefully defended by the laws, in their rights of character, and family, and property. If there is no way to adjust the scheme of legal process and record in our courts, but to regard the married woman as *femme covert*, existing in and under the name of her husband, and having no right of suit in her own name; there must yet be due provision made for the complete assertion of her personality, and the due protection of her property from every sort of encroachment, whether by her husband, or by wrong-doers acting in conspiracy with him. The law must be law for women, as truly as for men. Every thing must be so adjusted, if possible, as to remove the liabilities of wrong, and fortify the securities of right, and multiply the chances of industry for women. If we undertake to legislate for them, we must do better for them in favor, than they can propose, or dictate, or vote for themselves, and bow them gallantly forward into all best conditions and positions appropriate to their sex.

What then—for this is getting now to be the principal and most forward question—what are we to say or decide in respect to the question of suffrage for women? Does it follow that in doing all which is best, and for the highest possible advantage of women, we are called to give them an equal place with men in the ballot, and the right of public office? To this question we are now brought, and what I have been saying in this present chapter, has been specially designed to prepare it in such manner as to place it in the best condition for a just settlement.

Many persons who mistook their ground, in opposing the abolition of slavery, are naturally shy, under this new question, of being caught again,

and are half ready to leap into the gulf of what
is called the emancipation of women, before they
can distinctly see the bottom of it. Others again,
who have all their lives long meant to keep the
van of human progress and never fall behind, are
now being pushed on blindly by their mere habit,
as if there were some real inconsistency in turning
conservative now. They have a certain dislike
or distaste for any such holding back of motion,
and it troubles them that, for some reason, they do
not feel as ready to go forward as they would expect. The very great distinction between reforms
that go with nature, and reforms that go against
nature, they do not apprehend distinctly enough
to have the benefit of it. And just here lies the
question, we are now to see, of this very great, fearfully momentous question of women's suffrage.

It is amazing that so many of our writers and
debaters are able to handle this question so
lightly. For one, I am never able to look down
this gulf without a shudder of recoil. I read two
days ago in the "Nation" newspaper an article
headed, "*Is there such a thing as sex ?*"—the most
brilliant and really most complete utterance I have
anywhere met, and to which I may perhaps recur
hereafter—but there was a single point in the
conception of it which I could not see, and felt to
be even dangerously false. The writer wanted us
to look on this matter tentatively; saying, in effect,
" go on, make approaches, carry out the reform

by stages, and make it sure, that you are not too far on your way, whenever you may wish to retrace your steps." But the terrible thing about this *revocare gradum* is that there is no such possibility. Women having once gotten the polls will have them to the end, and if we precipitate our American society down this abyss, and make a final wreck of our public virtue in it, that is the end of our new-born, more beneficent civilization. The race must now look for some other and second new world—where shall it be found—that can set on foot still another and better experiment. Our sun is set; is there any other sun to rise?

II.

NO RIGHT OF SUFFRAGE ABSOLUTE IN MAN OR WOMAN.

In a campaign raised for women's suffrage, it was to be expected that the argument would take its beginning at our American doctrine of rights; or, as is sometimes put, of equal rights, natural rights, rights of natural equality. Probably the proposed reform itself is due to an over-absolute, uncritical reception of that doctrine; being only a fair extension, or logically right version of it. However this may be, the advocates of women's suffrage are quite innocent, doubtless, of any suspicion that these and other like phrases, current in our green age of statesmanship, are more pretentious than solid, and take us more by their sound than by any properly discovered meaning. And they have as good right to hold them in faith, and draw them into their particular applications, as many others have to hold them in the same faith, and yet eschew the applications.

If we desire to know exactly what merit or meaning there may be in these famous declarations of rights, equalities, compacts, consentings of the governed through majorities, and the like, we must take the lesson where the lesson was first taken. After long ages of priestcraft and princecraft in royal and noble families, ages of wrong and crushing absolutism, under pretext even of divine right, certain forward minds began to be stirred with a natural detestation. They were such men as Rousseau and Voltaire and others, sometimes called malignants; otherwise, philosophers, free-thinkers, agitators for liberty. They hated government—royalty that is, and aristocracy--as a shocking insult and fraud, and hated religion as the stupendous lie that seasoned and sanctified the fraud; assuming that what they saw of government was government, and what they saw of religion was religion. Full of this immense disgust, they betook themselves mentally to the woods, and began to envy the people of the woods. Savage life—this they called the paradise, and they even seemed to picture it with a true longing. Here are no distinctions but the simple equality of nature, the virtues are unsophisticated, the religion is nature, government, if they have it, is a matter of simple consent and compact.

The picture had such fascination to them and to thousands far away, in sympathy with them, that a kind of general effort began, to conceive a doctrine of the state, that was in fact a doctrine of the woods. The new philosophy, or new liberty began thus at the condition of nature; under taking to show how men, qualified and set on by the promptings of nature, could originate a state of civil order and obligatory law. The problem was to create obligation from below that is not from above; such as will stand firm and sure, apart from any terms of divine order or sanctions of divine magistracy. The government that was to be, must be contributed by the consent of the governed, and as the governed are all mere natural men, standing on that footing of equality—as they do in the woods—their consent is in their vote, and their vote is grounded in their equal right to vote. And so, out of mere nature, and built up from below, there is to be raised a complete civil order, binding on each citizen—no thanks to God— because the general citizenship so orders and decrees. Sometimes the scheme is further elaborated by showing that all right government so made, is in fact a "social compact;" where the multitude come in to surrender enough of their individual right and liberty, to make up a pool of endowment for the state. A whole system of phraseologies came into use in this manner that belonged to the general type of the free-thinking philosophy, and fell into such currency in speech that multitudes received the mixture without knowing at all whence it came. Even the really great mind of Locke took in somewhat of the infection, without being duly aware of the sophistry and dangerous falsity covered up under these pretentious guises.

In this way it came to pass that our fathers of the American revolution, long ago taken by these catch-words of liberty, fell into their use, more easily than was to be desired, in their manifestoes and public declarations. And the phraseologies thus adopted were what Mr. Choate very properly, though to the mortal offense of many, called "the glittering generalities." They are just what led Mr. Calhoun into his miserably delusive state-rights sophism, where he infers that if government is founded in consent, then it is an agency or trust contributed by the parties, and therefore terminable by them. Bitterly have we paid for this very cheap imposture of philosophy, in our late dreadful war of rebellion, and now it is to be seen, whether it may plunge us again down this other, deeper gulf of women's suffrage.

The short argument, as it is commonly put, runs thus: women are the equals of men, and have therefore an equal right to vote. In which very brief and very simple form of deduction, there are, if we are not willing to be taken by the shallowest possible fallacies, two quite plainly untrue conclusions. First, it is not certainly true that women are equal to men. They are equally women as men are men; they are equally human as men; they are so far equally entitled to protection as men, but it does not hence appear that they are equal to men. They may be superior to men; they may be inferior to men; but what is a great deal closer probably to the truth, they may be very unlike in kind to men; so unlike that in the civil state they had best, both for their own sake and for the public good, stand back from any claim of right, in the public administration of the laws. How far this unlikeness extends is not here the question. I shall undertake, at a future stage of the discussion, to state more precisely in what the relative unlikeness consists; for the present I cannot forbear citing from the *Nation*, a very short but excellently vigorous statement of the fact itself. "The unlikeness between men and women is radical and essential. It runs through all the spheres. Distinct as they are in bodily form and features, they are quite as distinct in mental and moral characteristics. They neither think, feel, wish, purpose, will, nor act alike. They take the same views of nothing. The old statements that one is passive, the other active; one emotional, the other moral; one affectionate, the other rational; one sentimental, the other intellectual, are likely to be more than verified by science. Of course, these statements, whether verified or not, do not justify the imposition of arbitrary limits on opportunity or enterprise. It still remains to determine what place each can fill, what work each can do, what standard each can reach; and these nature should be left to determine. But that both can not occupy the same place, do the same work, or reach the same standard, ought, we think, to be assumed. Nature has decreed it so." Accordingly, if the two sexes are so very unlike in *kind*, there can, so far, be no predication of equality between them. And then, just so far, the argument for a right in women to vote, in consideration of their equality, is inconclusive. We do not say that a yard is equal to a pound, because the two measures have no common quality; though it may be that a yard of some one thing is equal in value to a pound of some other. We do not say, taking an example where there is more appearance of a common quality, that silk and flax are equal; and yet they may make an equally strong, or equally fine thread; but since one will make a finer lace, and the other a more splendid robe, one a superb damask, and the other a superb velvet, we do not think of saying at all, that they are equal, because they are so far different in kind. In which also we may see, that, while women and men have a great many common properties, they have also a great many which are not common— so many, that we never can be sure what we mean by it, when we say that they are equal.

Yes, but their rights are equal, some will hasten, it may be, to answer, and that is enough to support the argument. Doubtless they have a perfect and complete right to be women, as men have to be men, but it may be, still, that the having a perfect right to be either women or men, does not include any right of voting at all—that is the very question here in issue.

The second fallacy above referred to is built on an argument equally baseless; it is that, being equal to men, women have a right to vote because men have a right to vote. Here the meaning is, if there is any, that men have a natural right to vote, or a right to vote that is grounded in nature. The words *man* and *suffrage* have, in this view, a fixed relation; a universal and permanent relation; such that suffrage never was or can be denied them, save by a public wrong; for every right is a something never to be stripped away, except by a wrong. Since, then, prior to the arrival of our own American Republic, there had never been more than two or three small peoples in the world that acknowledged any right to vote at all, and these no equal right, but only rights so unequal that a very few men of grade, as in Rome, counted more than a whole bottom tier of rabble that composed the chief population of the city, we are seen to have begun our public history, by assuming that there never before had been a legitimate government in the world! If we could say that, and not be shocked by the nonsense of our assumption, we were certainly a very remarkable people. How much better and closer to the sound realities of history, to have confessed, that all the great monarchies, and the rising and falling, and dawning and vanishing, and even the merely *de facto* states, had a certain morally incipient and legitimate authority, even though they gave no right of voting at all, and never heard or even thought of such a thing. Besides, we had not then, and never since have had, ourselves, any equal right of voting as being men, saying nothing of women, under our own constitutions and liberties. Some of us have been voting on the score of our property; some on the right we have bought by military service; some on the ground of qualifications imparted by our education; some on the count of our slaves. Doubtless we that are males are all so far equal, but we never to this day have been allowed to vote on our naked equality, except in here and there a single State. How then does it fare with the argument that women have a right, on the score of their equality with men, when men themselves can not vote on the score of their own equality with one another? Besides, if any of us think to make out a natural right of voting, whether in men or women, a sufficient hunt of our psychologic nature ought to find some place in it where the right, for so many ages undiscovered, inheres. It was observed, long ages ago, by such men as Plato, Aristotle, Cicero, and others, that our very nature is configured, all through, to the civil state, and the condition of civil obligation;

but no man has ever yet discovered that there is a right to vote twisted in among our functions and rational categories. When that discovery is made, it will be as soon as any such natural right can be set in account, and made a basis of argument for the voting of women.

Whence then do we get what now we call the right to vote? If it is not grounded in our nature, whence comes it? Some will imagine that the payment of taxes involves a right of representation, and this a right of voting; so that we have a good title to the suffrage made up indirectly. But the right of representation—who has ever imagined, till quite recently, that such a right must accrue on the payment of taxes, and that no government is legitimate which does not allow that right? How little government has there been in the world that had even a thought of representation as connected with taxation?—has there been no government, therefore, but only wrong? It may be desirable, I grant, since the people are taxed, that they should have some check upon the taxing power, and some voice in the public appropriation of money. But that is a matter which belongs to a consideration of measures and regulations, and not in any sense to first principles. Our fathers in the revolution had a great deal to say of being taxed by the Parliament without being represented in it, and seemed almost to hang the vindication of their revolt on this one point of grievance. But there was a peculiarity in their protest which neither they nor we have always observed, as distinctly as the due understanding of it requires. It was really a protest against having this great, new world farmed and used, for the benefit of a little, far-off patch of island in the German Ocean, which, compared with the gigantic world-empire here in debate, had no consequence and could have no continental future at all. On this canvass of outspreading futurity it was, that so many vehement protestations, indignations, and threats, cast their shadows. The real meaning was that such and so great a people are not to be kept for the fleece! And yet these same colonial fathers and patriots were every year taxing thousands, both of men and women, without any thought of a wrong, in not giving them a chance of representation. And if, afterward, they discovered that their argument could rightly be extended, so as to include the relations of individual persons to the state, they did not even then discover, and it is not to this day discovered, that women paying taxes have, by consequence, a right of representation. All that we can now say is that it stands before us as a question to be debated, whether it will be for their benefit and for the public good, that women be partakers also in the right of suffrage and of representation? It is not a question of absolute right or first principle, as when the right of conscience is asserted; for then there is no point to be debated; but it is a question of benefit concerned or not concerned, in a certain political measure—that, and nothing more. In the admission of men to a right of suffrage, it has never been voted for any one absolute reason. Sometimes it has been because they are taxed, sometimes because they are liable to be, sometimes because they perform military duty, sometimes because it discourages or takes away hope from their virtue not to allow it, sometimes because the refusal awakens animosities in them against the state. So if women ever have the right of voting accorded to them, it must be for a like variety of reasons, and not on the ground of any absolute principle.

What then becomes, some will ask, of the great law of consent, that in which we affirm "that governments instituted among men derive their just powers from the consent of the governed." That may be true, or partly true, I answer in some possible sense of the terms, but never as an absolute proposition. It may be true enough sometimes to be asserted antagonistically with great advantage; as where there is really wanted some limit, or countercheck for the due restraining of power. But if it be meant that no government is legitimate, save as it has the actual consent of its people, then there have been very few legitimate governments. Nay, there never has been one, and is not now. No fifth part of our own people, in fact, ever consented to the government, whether formally or by implication.

No new statute passed, ever had the consent of more then a very small fraction of the people. Minors, women, invalids, absentees, voters of the opposing party—take away all these, and how much of consent is left? If the major vote of such as have the ballot supposes general consent, then it must be by a legal fiction so great, that it would scarcely be greater without any vote at all.

If it be meant that all just powers of government are derived from the consent of the governed, in the sense, that so many "just powers" are, in fact, gotten by the surrender and contribution of rights belonging to individuals—an argument very often stated and by many soberly believed—then it is in point to answer that no civil right, or power, ever belonged, or, by any possible supposition, could belong, to any individual, or multitude of individuals. Has any individual a right to make arrests, a right to enforce contracts, a right to put contending parties on trial for the settlement of their disputes, a right of imprisonment, or penal enforcement, or making war or peace; a right, in one word, to exercise the least authority, or law-giving power over society? In this particular sense of the terms, we are rather to say that no one just power of government was ever derived, or ever could be, from the consent of the governed.

There is nothing, therefore, to be gained for women's suffrage, under this principle, as the champion debaters of the sex are often heard to assume. Women must get their right to vote, if at all, just where men have gotten it; out of history, out of providential preparations and causes, out of the concessions of custom, out of expediences concluded, and debated reasons of public benefit. We have no better right than this, as men, and there is no better right to be, for women. The question is concluded for them, by no *a priori* matter, but it is their right and privilege to show, that a power to hold office and vote will be for the real benefit of their sex, and for the solid and permanent good of society. Indeed, if they can only make it appear that they themselves will be put in a more favorable condition of life and character, by thus opening the political arena to them, we shall even deem the controversy, if there be a controversy, to be effectually ended. If we sometimes oppress them by our heedlessness, it is our custom rather, in matters of deliberate purpose, to give them more than will be either for their benefit or our own.

Having argued in this manner the question of right, showing that suffrage is a right given, never a right to be demanded because it inheres beforehand in the person, and that neither men nor women have any title to it, save what is grounded in considerations of benefit, I am tempted to add another clause and topic in the argument, just for the purpose of taking down a little our egregious opinion of the suffrage. The transcendent merit we assume for our institute of free suffrage is not quite as evident as we think it is; far less evident than our women think it is, when they look to find a new-creation stage of advancement in it. In a certain large view, it has done bravely for us, and we have much to boast in it; which we do not forget to boast, in terms, that far exceed all rational proportions of merit, and even display some tokens of national conceit. After all, our free suffrage state, when taken close at hand, as when we go to the ballot, makes a rather coarse, half nasty element; where men are pitched into count, without any consideration of merit or weight, and where they vote promotions, with only the feeblest, mere chance reference to the merit of the promotions voted. The machinery is dreadfully loose, and the look of order and right is only what a pell-mell operation yields. We are coaxed and flattered, for the time, by the feeling that we are doing something great, and getting a more advanced consequence in it. But, for one, I seriously doubt whether any so great benefits, either personal or public, are coming out of the suffrage, as we are wont to assume. It certainly can make the corruptest, most intolerable government in the world; as it is rapidly finding how to do already in the city of New York, and it is plainly to be seen that possible evils are covered up in it, that may finally take us down backward, faster than its former benefit has sent us onward. That it has a law of limitation in its own nature, and will come to its end and disappear within a comparatively short run of time, is far more probable than some of us suppose.

I speak in this manner, having distinctly in mind a certain way of promotion established in one of the great nations of the world, that has a far superior dignity and much better promise both of permanence and character. Instead of electing by suffrage, it elects by contest; that is, by trials of merit and personal qualification. It works by the West Point method, and hangs promotion at the end, on the scale of merit discovered. The whole grand nation, comprising four hundred millions of people, is a West Point cadetship extended. The humblest as well as the highest of the youth, are put in schooling, and then are sifted three times over, by three great examinations that go up by an ascending series. And then, out of the very limited number of the cadets that are crowned at the last, are to come all the high officers of the kingdom—officers to be who will be known as long as they live, to have excelled, first, in scholarship; secondly, in talent and capacity of writing; and thirdly, in the well-attested record of an upright, pure behavior. Our contempt for this Chinese people had better be expended fast, for we shall not have our opportunity long. A nation that existed a thousand years before the Trojan

THE REFORM AGAINST NATURE. 47

war, came to its full type in the days of Pericles, and still holds on as by some gift of civil immortality, well and most systematically governed still, with less of fraud, injustice, and official peculation in its magistracies than we have in ours, and a great deal less of crime, and a great deal more both of industry and high morality in its people than we are able to claim in our own, is not despisable, except by ignorance. Their only misfortune is that they have been too stringently educated; chained fast, in that manner, to the classic lore of their fathers, and kept back from the progressive studies of natural science; but already they are creating great universities to repair the deficit. And their fearfully intense scholarship will put .them very soon at our side in all the modern ideas, sciences, and improvements, and they will stand forth in their new great future only the more conspicuous, that they have had so grand a past. And God forbid that they ever be so far captivated by our dreadfully inferior, cheap way of suffrage, as to give up their cadetship way of promotion for it; a plan that has put the whole nation climbing upward, and will keep it climbing, to the end of the world—only climbing the more rapidly and surely now, that it has gotten new springs of life and self-renewing order. Emerging in this manner into modern ideas, and a modern career, China will, by this time, be the supreme world-wonder of history and historic empire, and the clumsy and coarse figure we make in .our half-

qualified magistracies chosen by suffrage, will
not be as impressive as most of us would like to
believe. Though perhaps it will comfort us a
little, that these people of China do themselves
maintain a suffrage in a certain lower plane of life,
where it makes a kind of volunteer department
for their benefit. They choose a class of elders,
so called, who are, in fact, a board of referees for
settling their controversies, and helping them
maintain their rights when oppressed by wrongs
and exactions of the state officers. They are no part
of the government any more than arbitrators, or a
vigilance committee, would be with us; and yet
the government allows their choice to simplify its
own immense complexities, and bring the people
help in what would also be theirs.

I have sketched this outline, not exactly required by the argument, simply because a considerable dose of humility is needed visibly, to cure us of the nonsense, which having first infected our men with undue conceit of advancement, is now infecting our women with as unreal and excessive hope that they may win the same. There is much less for us all here than our coarse patriotic fervors assume, and a great deal less for women than for men. If the scheme of suffrage must go down, it will be a very great advantage that our women are not in it. It will go down, if at all, simply by the rotting process of its own corruptions, and our ambitious women will find little comfort in being the bad other half that goes down with it.

THE REFORM AGAINST NATURE. 49

III.

WOMAN NOT CREATED OR CALLED TO GOVERN.

It was a point made, in the brief chapter preceding, that no argument for women's suffrage, based on the equality, or equally human property of women with men, can have more than a show of validity; for the reason that men and women are, to some very large extent, unlike in kind; and it may be so far unlike, as to forbid any rational comparison as respects equality; and, of course, to forbid any such inference of right for women because that right is accorded to men. It becomes, in this view, a matter of consequence to inquire whether the supposed unlikeness of kind includes matters of distinction that amount to a proper disqualification, or which really forbid, as contrary to nature, the extension of any such political right to women.

It is not to be denied that women are made in the image of God as truly as men, having faculties and categories of mind that are equal in number, and so far similar in kind, as to pass under the same general names. What is right and true to one sex, is right and true also to the other. They think by the same laws, they perceive, and judge, and remember, and will, and love, and hate, in the exercise of functions that compose personalities psychologically similar, however different in degree, and however differently tempered, fibered, tensified, and toned for action. In a word, they are equally human, and compared with orders of being above and below them are of the same kind. And yet in their relationship of sex, within their own human order, they are so widely different, nevertheless, that the distinction never misses observation. Their very personality, which even seemed identical in the inventory, taking on sexhood, becomes broadly differential in that fact, and submits to a deep-set, dual classification.

A mere glance at the two sexes, externally related, suggests some very wide distinction of mold whatever it be. The man is taller and more muscular, has a larger brain, and a longer stride in his walk. The woman is lighter and shorter, and moves more gracefully. In physical strength the man is greatly superior, and the base in his voice and the shag on his face, and the swing and sway of his shoulders, represent a personality in him that has some attribute of thunder. But there is no look of thunder in the woman. Her skin is too finely woven, too wonderfully delicate to be the rugged housing of thunder. Her soft, upper octave voice, her small hands, her features played as in quality and not for quantity, her complexion played as if there were a principle of beauty living under it—there is abundance of expression here, as many great, proud souls of heroes have been finding in all ages, but it is unOlympic as possible in kind. Glancing thus upon man, his look says, Force, Authority, Decision, Self-asserting Counsel, Victory. And the woman as evidently says, "I will trust, and be cherished, and give sympathy and take ownership in the victor, and double his honors by the honors I contribute myself." They are yet one species, but if they were two, they would be scarcely more unlike. So very wide is the unlikeness, that they are a great deal more like two species, than like two varieties. Their distinction of sex puts them in different classes of being, only they are classes so nearly unified by their unlikeness, that they compose a whole, so to speak, of humanity, by their common relationship. One is the force principle, the other is the beauty principle. One is the forward, pioneering mastery, the out-door battle-ax of public war and family providence; the other is the in-door faculty, *covert*, as the law would say, and complementary, mistress and dispenser of the enjoyabilities. Enterprise and high counsel belong to one, also to batter the severities of fortune, conquer the raw material of supply; ornamentation, order, comfortable use, all flavors, and garnishes, and charms to the other. The man, as in fatherhood, carries the name and flag; the woman, as in motherhood, takes the name on herself and puts it on her children, passing out of sight legally, to be a covert nature included henceforth in her husband. They are positivity and receptivity, they are providence and use, they are strength and beauty, they are mass and color, they are store-house and table, they are substance and relish, and nothing goes to its mark or becomes a real value till it passes both.

But we are dealing, so far, in this outward delineation of the sexual distinctions, in matters general, and have not taken up, as yet, the more particular matter at issue in our question of suffrage. The precise point here to be observed, is that masculinity carries, in the distribution of sex, the governmental function. The forwarding force, the brave-and-dare element, whether toward nature or against human opposers, the responsible engineering of place and work and calling, all determinations outward, whether toward enemies, or among causes, or in ventures of commerce, or in diplomatic treaties and warlike relations of peoples, belong to man and to what may be called his manly prerogative. That is, man is to govern; all government belongs to men. Not that women are never set in kingly positions to represent, or personate the kingly power; of that I shall speak hereafter in another place. For the present, I simply remark, that the authority they wield in such cases is only what the masculine traditions put upon them, or into them, when they are used to fill the gaps of kinghood, by maintaining the court pageantries and the royal signature; they do not reign as kings do by an authority that is largely personal in themselves. Were they obliged to maintain themselves in that way, it would very soon be discovered how little authority there is in women. We take pleasure not seldom in allowing women to rule us by the volunteering deference we pay to their womanhood; we often talk of our loyalty to the sex; but we never see the woman who can hold a particle of authority in us by her own positive rule or the emphasis of her own personality.

To prevent misunderstanding it may be proper to say that I am not asserting a right here in men to bolt upon women, wives for example, in the peremptory way of command; I am only asserting the natural leadership, the decision-power, the determinating will of the house and the state, as belonging to men. Certain engineering questions, for example, must be settled, the question of expenditure as related to income, the question of residence, occupation, emigration; where of course every endeavor should be made to compose differences of feeling and judgment, and settle points by agreement. But if a case arises, where agreement is impossible, one of the two, clearly, must decide, and it must be the man. The woman's law of allegiance, sometimes a hard one, requires it of her to adhere to the man, submit herself to his fortunes, and go down with him bravely, when his day of disaster comes. The sway, the determinating mastership, must so far be with him, and it can not be anywhere else, without some very deplorable consequences to his manhood. If he has no sway-force in him equal to this, no authority of will and council that enables him to hold the reins, he is no longer what nature means when she makes a man. And the refractory woman who has so far balked his manhood will have honored herself quite as little as him.

Happily, it is just as natural to women to maintain this beautiful allegiance to the masterhood and governing sway-force of men, both in the family and the state, as we could wish it to be. Nothing, in fact, is more touching than to see how far they will go, how much they will bear, how absurdly persist in dressing up the masculine idol they have undertaken to crown, or exalt. They do no such thing toward other women, they totally disown the authority of women, and can not even think it possible for women to preside in their assemblies. They do not ask, it may be, how, or why it is that they insist on having a man to preside? but if they could see the reason, as it lies in the inner feeling, they would discover in it a most complete refutation of their claim of suffrage itself. Looking on their chairman—a man, and

THE REFORM AGAINST NATURE. 55

why a man?—they would confess that, by that sign, their very cause is convicted of incongruity. Or if it occurs to them to urge, in excuse, that women have no experience in the ordering of assemblies, they can be more easily qualified, than they can to make a speech. They are, some of them, quick enough to learn Jefferson's Manual quite through, in half a day. Probably enough, too, the man they have chosen, never before presided over an assembly in his life.

Now the right of suffrage as demanded for women, is itself a function of government. Besides, it contemplates also, as an integral part of the proposed reform, that women should be eligible to office. For if this were not conceded, we know perfectly beforehand, that the women voters would so wield their balance of power as to conquer the right of office in a very short time. All office must, of course, be open to them, as certainly as the polls are open. Indeed they sometimes take the jubilant mood even now, in their anticipation of the day, when they will have their seat in Congress, on the bench of justice, in the President's cabinet, and why not in the chair of the Presidency itself? when the missions abroad, the collectorships, the marshal and police functions, will be theirs, and finally, the heroic capabilities of women so far discovered, as to allow them a place in the command of fleets and armies, and full chance given their ambition, to win, as for solid history, what many call the mythic honors of a Semiramis or a Deborah.

The claim put forward then is, and will be commonly allowed to be, a claim of authority; a claim by women to govern, or be forward in the government of men; wherein they deny, in fact, a first distinction of their sex. The claim of a beard would not be a more radical revolt against nature. It says: "give us force, give us the forward right, give us authority, let us take our turn also at the thunder." Just contrary to this, I feel obliged to assert the natural subordination of women. They are put under authority by their nature itself, and if they will not take it as their privilege to be, if they call it insult and oppression, they set a character on their position which no man could; they put contempt themselves on their womanhood. Indeed, their very claim of suffrage on the ground of their equality with men, ignores just what is most distinctive in their kind, and is neither more nor less than a challenge of the rights of masculinity. And the harshest thing that can be said of their reform would be, that they mean it as it is.

Asserting in this very decisive manner the natural submission of women, and their very certain lack, whether as respects the right or the fact, of authority, it will seem to many, as I very much fear, to be a harsh, or even a rude and coarse attack upon their sex. If it is so taken, it certainly need not be. We Americans take up some very crude notions of subordination, as if it implied inferior quality, character, power. No such thing is true, or less than plainly false. Subordination is one thing, inferiority an immensely different thing. Subordinate as they are, in their naturally sheltered relation, I seriously doubt whether we should not also assert their superiority. They do quite as much, and I strongly suspect, more for the world. Their moral nature is more delicately perceptive. Their religious inspirations, or inspirabilities, put them closer to God, as having a more celestial property and affinities more superlative. It may be that men have larger quantity in the scale of talent, while yet they are enough coarser in the grain of their quality to more than balance the score.

Quality of brain, whatever we may say of size, can not be less than a matter of chief significance, and the fiber of a woman's brain is likely to be as much finer as the fiber of her skin; capable also, for that reason, of a more delicately feeling and bright insight, a more dramatic fancy-play, and a facility and grace of movement far more closely related to beauty. And who of us, making due account of the late admirable works of genius presented by our women authors, has not sometimes been taken hold of secretly by the question, whether finally a new age of literature is not coming on the world, in the mental unfolding of this other hitherto but half-discovered half of the race. Or if we talk of inspirations and the inspired forces of genius, have we no reason to imagine that, when the more divinely impregnate thought of the womanly souls is born, we shall see a divine daughterhood that has more than sonship in it, a finer and more glorifiable humanity. Mary herself—was she not subordinate to Joseph? But she was not therefore inferior.

And if we should be obliged, in this way, to admit that the womanly nature, all over the world, is instinctively submitted to the manly nature, must we for that reason judge that woman is less honored, less divinely gifted, lower in the scale of possibilities?

What are we doing in fact, even now and always, but submitting our manhood to her in another and different way of submission, that implies a tribute of homage more tenderly delicate and voluntary, and more beautiful to look upon than any that can possibly be rendered, either by her or by us, on the so much desired footing of equality. Equality! Great heaven! are we so blind as to think no beauty possible in these terms of sexhood, because they import relations of difference? Must humanity become a bin of seeds all just alike, before we can be patient with our part in it? And again, to make up the beauty and true interest of life, why should not our children insist on being born at a point past majority, with their teeth and beards already grown, and their old people's wisdoms ripened before experience? Why this odious, never to be endured inequality? How strange indeed, how cross to our best notions of justice, and of true social equity and beauty, that parents are born older than their children, getting rights that include no equal vote at all, and that vary in as many grades and colors as the fit care and discipline of so many ages require.

But there is an aspect of privilege, in this matter of subordination, which, instead of inferring the inferiority of women, gives them, when morally considered, the truest and sublimest conditions of ascendency. The highest virtues, purest in motive and really most difficult, are never to be looked for in the most forward and potentially regnant states. They belong rather to the subject conditions, where the coarse admixtures of pride and worldly power are shut away. We get the true analogy here in the great domain of nature, where the coarse and forceful causes seem to be doing every thing, and yet, in all finest, truest estimates of power, do comparatively nothing. The sun blazes and burns, the volcanoes burst and bury cities with ashes, the earthquakes rock and rend, the comets blaze on the sky, and the fierce windstorms tear it; and these and such like make up, as we think, the supreme causes to which all the humblest ingredients of our landscapes are of course inferior. And yet, if we come to the true scale of honors gotten upon human feeling, or in it, these same humbler, these inferior things of the landscapes are, in fact, immensely superior, and the others have but a hundredth part of the significance. The dews, the grasses, the green life of the trees, the fragrant breath of the mornings, the sunset colors on the clouds and the hills, the springs that break out under them, and the brooks leaping down their slopes, the songs of the birds, the feeding of cattle in their pastures—the inventory is a long one; who can tell what is in it, or how much? This only we know, that the great world-forces holding sway and swinging above are scarcely appreciable, in comparison with the finer things of beauty they subordinate. We do not half as much respect or feel the dominating forces of the world as we do the dominated graces. Or if certain gross, coarse-judging souls, will think great things are done for them only by causes that bruise and batter, and that other things subordinate to these are of course inferior, these latter still will not be inferior even to them. After all, the woman things of the world, the patient-working, unobtrusive, graceful causes will be doing more.

Under this analogy, we perceive how force, by its own nature, always and of course subordinates beauty. And it is just as true in things moral and spiritual as in things natural. Only they that are humble can be exalted; only the last can be first. The highest, finest molds of good, are grown only

in the lowliest and most subject conditions. Was
Mary inferior because she was a lowly, subject
woman? Was her holy thing, her son, inferior
because he was subject, in his beautiful childhood,
and subject all his life long, down to the last
hour's breath and the last nail driven? Many have
imagined that they discovered in Jesus both a
manly and a womanly nature, and that he became
the perfect one, because in this union he was able,
in so great force and authority, to bear so many
things with a gentle submission and an unfaltering patience.

There can not, in this view, be a greater mistake,
or one that indicates a coarser apprehension, than
when our women, agitating for the right of suffrage,
take it as an offense against their natural equality,
that they are not allowed to help govern the
world. It is as if the gentle mignonnette and violet were raised in protest against the regal dahlia,
when they are in truth a great deal more potentially regnant themselves. What do these women
ask, in fact, but to be weighed in the gross weight-scales of force, making nothing of that higher,
finer nature, by which God expects it of them to
flavor the world. They must govern, they must
go into the fight, they must bruise and batter
themselves—what are they equal to, if they are
not equal to men? As if it were nothing, a little
way back, after all the coarse things of the world
are done, to govern, by graces, the men that gov-

ern by forces, and go through family and country, and the times, with a ministry more powerful, finer in the motive, less mixed with selfishness and will, and just as much closer to the really celestial type of good. God save us from the loss of this better, almost divinely superior ministry; for lost it will assuredly be, when our women have come down to be litigators with us in the candidacies, contests, and campaigns of political warfare. Still life is then no more, and the man who goes home at night from his caucus fight, or campaign speech, goes in, not to cease and rest, but to be dinned with the echo, or perhaps bold counter-echo of his own harsh battle. The kitchen dins the parlor, and one end of the table dins the other. Upstairs, down-stairs, in the lady's chamber—every where the same harsh gong is ringing, from year to year. Oh! if we could get away! how many will then say it, and pray it—into some bright corner where yet there are true women left—women with soft voices, shrilled by no brassiness or dinging sound of party war!

Why, if our women could but see what they are doing now, what superior grades of beauty and power they fill, and how far above equality with men they rise, when they keep their own pure atmosphere of silence, and their field of peace, how they make a realm into which the poor bruised fighters, with their passions galled, and their minds scarred with wrong—their hates, disappointments, grudges, and hard-worn ambitions—may come in, to be quieted, and civilized, and get some touch of the angelic, I think they would be very little apt to disrespect their womanly subordination. It will signify any thing but their inferiority. If they are already taken with the foolish ambition of place, or of winning a public name, they may not be satisfied. But in that case they barter for this honor a great deal more than they can rightly spare. God's highest honors never go with noise, but they wait on silent worth, on the consciousness of good, on secret charities, and ministries untainted by ambition. Could they but say to the noisy nothings of this bribery, "Get thee hence, Satan," as Christ did to the same coarse nonsense of flattery, they would keep their subject-way of life as he kept his, and would think it honor enough that they also came not to be ministered unto, but to minister. And if it be the question for them, whether it is better to be classed in privilege with Jesus the subject, or with Cæsar the sovereign, it should not be difficult to decide.

Thus far we go in the principle that women are made to be subordinate, and men to be the forward operators and dominating authorities of the world. They have another field, where their really finer qualities and more inspirable gifts may get full room and scope for the most effective and divinest offices of life. Indeed we do not evenly set the balance of the question, if we do not say that woman has her government as truly as man, only it is not political, not among powers, and laws, and public causes. He governs from without downward, and she from within upward, and though there be a great difference of kind between our two words master and mistress, using this latter in its true, good sense, there is not a whit more of control signified, when we say that the man is the mastering power of the woman, than that she is the mistressing power of the man. He is at a point of sway more coarse, direct, and absolute—more nearly akin to force. She is at a point where she captivates the force, by a beautiful and right enjoyment of it, takes possession of the man, property, and soul, and will, and calling, and makes him joyfully her own. If the cases were inverted, he would make a coarse, awkward figure doubtless in the mistressing kind of government; but if we are to agitate for equality, why should he not have the beautiful chance given him of being a mistress-power in life—on the score of equality, even as she obtains a mastering power in life, when she obtains the suffrage.

As regards this right of priority and pioneering headship in man, and the so far subordinate and subject state in woman, implying still no superiority in him, and more than possible superiority in her, we have another illustration furnished by religion, that to such as have a true insight of the Christian plan or economy, will be strikingly apt and impressive. I refer to what is called the *law* and the *gospel*, as mutually related to each other. The law, which is the man, goes before, rough-hewing the work of government. It is Sinai-like, and speaks in thunder. It commands, and, by sanctions of force, where force is wanted, vindicates its own supreme authority. It so far has priority in rule, that it never can have any thing less; for the cessation of law is the cessation of government, and if it should only fall into second place or equal place with any thing else, it would lose the inherent sovereignty of its nature, when, of course, it can be law no longer. The gospel, meantime, coming after in order is the woman. It is subject as gospel to the husband, that is, to the law; it is made under the law; and the whole historic operation, by which it is organized, is itself obedience, submission, love, and sacrifice. And it is so perfectly subject to the law, that it professes nothing but a fulfillmen tof the law, and a universal recovery to it. Setting up for equality with law, or for itself, as having good right to assert and advance itself, is never so much as thought of; if it can but write the law on the heart of transgressors, all its wifely ends or ambitions are answered. And this it is supposed to do, by what is called grace; that is, by a way of approach so gentle, so winsome, and lovely, and close to the manner of true womanly grace, as to be another, more effective, side of the divine power; that which is the power of God unto salvation.

And now suppose the question to be raised, which of these is superior—works in the highest talent, does the greatest things, takes largest hold of the future, bears the loftiest inspirations, has most beauty of God in it, and really displays the finest, most etherealizing power? Undoubtedly it is the gospel. It goes above the law in doing every thing for it, and overtops it in glory, by submission to it. No power is in it, but the power of suffering and a subject state. It lives in sorrow and dies in sacrifice, and accomplishes just what the law, in "that it was weak," could not accomplish. The coarse ideas of force, and majesty, and all the pomps and thunders of enforcement are omitted here, and the simple wifehood of God's love, and beauty, is revealed, by what is lowliest and most dejected. And this is grace, the world-transforming grace in which God's empire culminates.

And yet our women will not have their subordinate, or subject state, because it makes them inferior! They want, alas! the culture of soul that is wanted to see the superiority to which they are elected. They come in the wedding grace of their Cana, or the suffering grace of their Calvary, and insist on their right to be Sinai, and play the thunders too themselves. "Give us also power," they say; and power to them is force, or an equal right of command. A most miserable and really low misconception, if only they had grace to see it. Here is their true power, in a disinterested and subject life of good. And there is a way in this to govern men, that is greatness itself and victory. What can the woman do that wants to vote, in order to be somewhat, but fume, and chafe, and tear, under what she calls the wrongs of her husband—so to make her weakness more weak, and her defeat more miserable—when if she could only consent to be true gospel and woman together, to be gentle, and patient, and right, and fearless, how certainly would she come out superior and put him at her feet. There seems to me, in this view, I confess, to be a something sacred, or angelic, in such womanhood. The morally grandest sight we see in this world is a real and ideally true woman. Send her to the polls if you will, give her an office, set the Hon. before her name, and by that time she is nobody.

As regards this question of suffrage, or the allowing of suffrage to women, there is yet another way of constructing the argument, which, though it may not be another, may be more convincing to some, viz. :—that the male and female natures together constitute the proper man, and are, therefore, both represented in the vote of the man. And the radical idea here assumed of the composite unity of the two, is attested, in fact, all over the world, in one form or another, and in different modes and degrees, whenever a marriage puts them in connection as husband and wife. The woman passes under shelter and protection, so far as even to drop her family name, and be only known under the family name of her husband. In the English common law she is said to be *femme covert*, a woman who is included, as respects all civil rights, in her husband. Her personality is so far merged in his, that she can not bring a suit any more in her own name, for it is a name no longer known to the law. The assumption is that, being in and of her husband, he will both act and answer for her, except when arraigned for crime. The Roman or civil law received by so many of the principal nations of the world, carries similar ideas with it, asserting the civil absorption of the wife in the husband in terms but slightly qualified.

The Russian law and the Chinese correspond. In all which we may see how close to nature runs the impression that woman is a complementary personality, and is rightly taken to exist in her husband, as she passes under his name in her marriage, and is consentingly covered by his protectorship.

Hence it is put forward by some, as the true answer to the claim of women's suffrage, that they are already represented in and by the vote of their husbands. But this again is only saying that they will be duly cared for and protected, by the voice their husbands have in government, when they do not govern for themselves. And nothing can be assumed more safely than that; for if by some *lache* of marital attention, helped by a certain natural gravitation toward injustice when attention sleeps, the laws may sometimes slip or subside into ways that bear oppressively on women, the wrong will be easily rectified. There is no deliberate willingness in men to oppress women; and as soon as any sufficient reminder comes, and a real grievance is shown, there is sure to be some adequate reform that redresses the wrong discovered. Our legislators, have abundantly shown their readiness, and even zeal, to remove every sort of harshness in the laws toward women; they make haste in it, and are willing even to go beyond the real equity and do, since it is for women, more than is equal, and more than they would ask legislating for themselves. If they want, indeed, a partial legislation, softer and more favorable than strict equality, their surest way to get it is to let it be the legislation of men. They will do any thing for women that has even a semblance of right.

What matter then is it, whether women have a representation by their own ballot or not? Perhaps it may better suit their ambition to be powers, than wards of the state, but it is a very fatuitous and really most unsentimental ambition. Oh! if we could only be assured as men, that we should be governed well, and safely defended in every right, secured in every privilege, without any representation at all, any right of suffrage, what better and more halcyon day of promise could heaven let down upon us. Such government would be like that of God·Himself. There is no privilege in representation, no inherent right of it in any state, save that, as rulers are themselves under evil, and prone to ways of wrong as God is not, it is convenient and imparts a feeling of security, to have the subjects themselves allowed a voice in the laws, and a part in their just enforcement. It is no first principle then, as our new state reformers assume, that women have a right of representation because they are human; in that way a right of suffrage; for nobody has any such right of representation, if only he can be well governed without such right; and women are as nearly sure of that as they can be, in the fact that they are made sure by the vote and representation of their husbands.

But they are many of them single persons, it may be urged, and have therefore no husbands by whose vote their rights may be protected. On this account too some of the opposers of women's suffrage, apprehending a defect in their argument based in the representative office of husbands, have conceded the right of widows and single women to vote; only requiring them to lose that right when they pass into the *femme covert* state.

But this would open a way for innumerable frauds, and confusions without end. Happily the whole cast of the argument is mistaken. Women are not changed in their nature, or in any natural right, because they are married. What we have to say is, that all women alike are made to be married, whether they are or not. The sex-nature of men and women is not altered by marriage, and according to that sex-nature, women are to be sheltered legally by men. Government is not given them, but protectors are given them, who are tender above all terms of equality. So that if it were necessary for them to be represented, and they had a right to be, the whole female order would be most effectively represented in the whole male order, without respect to any chances, or mischances, of marriage whatever.

And so there is to be secured for women a more benignant, softer kind of protectorship, which is bruised and battered by no contests, or made hard and imperious by no mere dominations of force. Of what use would government be, if all fine sentiments and gentle deferences and loyalties were killed by it? And there must be room for these in harbors and havens one side of the storms; where only soft winds blow, and silent atmospheres and breathings are allowed. The masculine half-being must be allowed to sink into the bigger self that he calls his home, and be sheltered in the womanly peace he has protected, for the gentler and more dear protection of his own more stormy life. Living only as male creatures in society with male, they would keep their pride, their will, their dry grudges, and self-seeking torments, and these would be their inventory. It is only when they take in the complementary graces of a domestic keeping—the carefulness, the love, the beauty—that they save moisture enough to fully and completely exist. That is the protectorship of men. This is the protectorship of women. And if the question be which is first in consequence, dearest, and most necessary, the women certainly shall say the first, and the men quite as certainly the last.

IV.

SCRIPTURE DOCTRINE COINCIDES.

Happily, we are not obliged to hang our opinions in this matter of women's suffrage on the moral expositions and dictations of Scripture; for the two points now made in respect to the natural subordination, or subject state, of women, and to the secondary, complementary office they hold in filling out the manhood of men, when merged politically in their protectorship, need no scriptural authority to support them. The Scripture has nothing to say of this matter, which is at all variant from what we see with our eyes. Indeed no scripture revelation, which at all disagrees with the bisexual facts of our existence as they are, could be true, or have any authority over the revelations made by such facts. The scripture revelations might interpret the revelations of nature, and let us farther into their meaning; or they might impart new disclosures that go farther and give us additional knowledge; but I do not see, in this particular case, that they do either. They seem to merely reiterate, and put in stronger emphasis, just what we learn by the sight of our eyes—that, and nothing more. However, a great many minds will revert almost instinctively here to what is given us by scripture authority, and will ask for the sentence it propounds as a final and determinate settlement, so far, of the questions in issue. Besides, we only pay a decent reverence to the teachings of God, when we bring our questions before this tribunal of divine authority and reason, as it is proposed in this chapter to do.

Coming, then, to the Word, what saith the Word? Take what view we please of the story of the creation, it scarcely matters as far as this particular subject is concerned; for the representation is, in any case, that the woman is created, not to be the man's re-duplication, or a second man, but to be the meet-helper of the man. She is to be a subsidiary nature, filling out the complete humanity of the man; and this fact is figured in a way of representation that makes her nature derivative from his, and so far of a quality at once cognate and complementary. "And Adam said, this is now bone of my bone and flesh of my flesh; she shall be called woman, because she was taken out of man. Therefore shall a man leave his father and mother, and cleave unto his wife, and they shall be one flesh."

So the parties stand in the scale of the creation. They are one flesh as being two, because one is the complement of the other. Then follows the precipitation of the fall, in which the composite unity becomes a bond of retributive liability, even as every other blessing is touched by the pangs of disorder. Before it was, " be fruitful and multiply;" now it is, to the subject party, " in sorrow shalt thou bring forth children; and thy desire shall be to thy husband, and he shall rule over thee." What before was only a protectoral relation, where the forward nature takes the subject into care and dear safe-keeping, is now to become a partly embittered relation, and be more or less galled by oppressions, such as wrong-doers in power will lay on the subject companions God gave to their protection. " Thy desire shall be to thy husband." This interprets no more the real order of nature, but the disorder of unnature; and how sadly and how heavy with sighing, all down the after ages, has the sentence been repeating its verifications; female nature suing, as it were, to male, and how often, alas! getting from even its love itself but a slack appreciation; sometimes burdens unstinted and weary homages of sorrow; sometimes only roughness and neglectful insolence. Visibly the man has precedence and the woman a subordinate lot, only it is no more the sweet relationship of order and protective sympathy originally intended, but of one made hard and dry by the partly retributive extirpations of love and tenderness. And still, under so many repulses and discouragements, the desire of the woman is, none the less fixedly, to the man and to his rule, harsh as it is now become in its severity, and dismally distempered by the abuse of power.

We descend across the ages to the times and declared maxims of the New Testament-era. Nothing, of course, is put down here to re-emphasize the retributions of sin, but the subordination of the woman to the man, and the complementary part she fills in the sheltered condition of her dependence, is, if possible, more emphatically stated. As "the head of every man is Christ," so "the head of the woman is the man;" as "he is the image and [reflected] glory of God," so "the woman is the glory of the man." "For the man is not of the woman, but the woman of the man. Neither was the man created for the woman, but the woman for the man." "The woman is to learn in silence, with all subjection"—"not to teach nor to usurp authority over the man, but to be in silence."

Now, these heavy pronouncements of the apostle come down with a kind of pounding emphasis on women, that sounds harshly. I should not dare to write in this way, and scarcely to think in this way, without adding something that is more appreciative and more delicately respectful both to merit and feeling. If Paul had been well married, that is, to such a wife as by character and personal attractions could make herself the mistress every wife should be, in the respectful homage of her husband, I think he would have learned some things about women which, in fact, he never did learn, and would have been as much more courteous and tenderly gracious in his words. And if he had lived in this particular age, I am not quite sure that he would have had as much to say of the obedience of women; for it will be observed that when he is speaking in this manner he is having respect almost always to "the shame" religion suffers when women are less patient, or less quietly subordinate, under the frequently domineering rule of their husbands, than the manner of the age requires. The point which has so great importance with him is, that Christian women shall not raise an accusation of scandal against the gospel, by the boldness of their liberty in the spirit and of their faith in Jesus. Of course Paul did not know every thing, whether about women or any other subject of knowledge. What the Spirit gave him he knew, and for all other kinds of knowledge he was on a footing with his age. And, in this view, doing justice to all that he positively declares, we are permitted to doubt whether he had a fully rounded conception of the finer and more superlative qualities of womanly talent. Do we not see, in fact, that womanly gifts are a great deal higher than his old-time habit and his mere bachelor acquaintanceship ever allowed him to know?

And yet he is perfectly right in every positive

utterance and moral pronouncement he makes.
So far he indorses and sanctions the grand first
truth of the sexly nature seen by us all; the superior headship of man, and the subordinated, complementary life of woman; and so the base note
of his music is rightly keyed. And, it must also
be said, in justice to his seemingly harsh and
somewhat overbearing dictations or casuistries,
that he does sometimes contrive to give a less despotic and more thoughtfully tender look to the
governing right of husbands. He does not say,
"Assert your rights and put your women in their
places," as he almost seemed to be doing just
now, but he says, "Husbands, love your wives,
even as Christ also loved the church, and gave
himself for it. So ought men to love their wives
as their own bodies. He that loveth his wife
loveth himself. For no man ever yet hated his
own flesh, but nourisheth and cherisheth it, even
as the Lord the church." In this most sacred
bond he conceives the two to be, in some sense,
two no more, a man and a woman, but "one
flesh" rather; practically unified, as in some mystic consolidation—even as Christ and the church
is made one by what he calls the "great mystery," their secret marriage bond in the Spirit. In
this bond, so truly sacred, let them both abide as
natures sealed for unity; "let every one of you, in
particular, so love his wife even as himself—[another self];—and the wife see that she reverence

her husband." He is husband still, and she is wife—their natural distinction remains—they only temper now the look of their relation, by as much as they soften the authority, to love on one side, and deepen the obedience, to reverence on the other.

Passing now to Peter who had been married, it is pleasant to see what his marriage has done for him, in the more appreciative manner of his writing. He begins at the same point with Paul —"Likewise ye wives be in subjection to your own husbands;" and the motive stated is one that encourages a confidence of power superior in some sense to the word of the gospel, and even to apostolic preaching itself, viz.: that their husbands may "without the word,"—without preaching, without exhortation—"be won by the conversation [the beautiful way] of their wives." In the same strain he goes on to speak of their adorning—which is to be no outward glare of trinkets, and gems, and braidings of hair, and dresses in the mode, as many think who count women only a toy—but it is to be internal worth and beauty, the hidden magic of a dear, celestial character; that which, in God's scale of judgment, is of great price. And I know not any thing ever said in Scripture of mortal beauty and perfection, which carries an impression so superlative as this word πολυτελες, all-perfect, precious, dear above price, and that "in the sight of the Lord;" as if it were conceived that a woman, dignified by such internal beauty, is really the finest mold of created being ever looked upon by even God himself.

Next, the apostle brings out another specially grand point in the behavior of Christian women, as related to the precedence and authority of their husbands, setting Sarah before them as the model of all finest dignity—"even as Sarah obeyed Abraham, calling him lord; whose daughters ye are when ye do well and are not afraid with any amazement." And if any thing will class a woman in her subject state with Christ himself in his, it will be that she is able to carry herself steadily through all the ungracious and violent and often fierce exactions of her lot, with a brave woman's heart, never cowed or driven out of courage by the tyrant her submission crowns. A delicate, defenseless, yet unfearing woman is a brave light! Her type of life is more like that of Christ than any man's can be, and so this rough-minded, impetuous, fisherman apostle evidently feels himself.

And, therefore, we are not surprised, when he goes on in the very next verse to exhort the "doing honor" to such women. Honor, as we commonly speak, is a kind of homage, such as inferiors pay to superiors, a subject nature to a governing nature. Rough apostle that he is, he is yet gallant enough to make a beautiful inversion here, calling on the husbands to give honor to the wives—the stronger vessel to the weaker and more fragile—and to take grade with them, so far, in the new love, as to be heirs together with them in the grace of life. He also intimates that if they can not do this, but must always be clamoring for equal rights on one side, or disowning the same on the other, their very " prayers will be hindered."

What now is the general result to which we are brought by this review of the Scripture, but that women are out of place in the governing of men. Even Comte himself does but echo the rejected word when he says, " Woman may persuade, advise, judge, but she should not command." The Scriptures have more delicate and genial ways of speaking often, than in some of the citations here made, but in whatever terms they speak, terms of cherishment, as for one's own body, or of love as to a second self, or of honor paid to the precious ornament of a beautiful soul, or of gallant deference and mindfulness to a person tenderly fragile, there is clearly never a thought that women have a claim, on any score, to be set forward as campaigners in the state with men. The assertion of their political equality with men would have shocked any apostle, or other scripture writer, and an agitation by women, based on such equality, to secure the right of open contest with men for political office and power, would have been looked upon even as an offense against nature itself—an outrage on decency and order utterly abominable. The great question of female suffrage they decide only the more effectually without naming it, for indeed it was a thing unknown, whether as respects the rights of men or of women, and we hear them say, just what we have been seeing with our eyes, that men are the force-element of the world, the imperative sex, and women the beauty-element, called to reign by the more sacred title of obedience and trust; both in unity, to be one flesh, a complemented whole of ornament and strength.

About the only aspect of equality, or likeness of kind between the two sexes, anywhere presented in the Scriptures, relates to the future life, where, we are told, they "neither marry nor are given in marriage, but are as the angels of God in heaven." And the declaration appears to be still more significant, when taken as connected with the fact that no scripture *angel* is put in the feminine gender, and that the word angel itself has no feminine. All which, as some may argue, tokens the fact, that sex belongs here below, and that both sexes alike have the real staple in them of a common angelhood in the life to come—which staple of course pertains to them as truly here, and makes them equal here as there.

The argument will be far-fetched of course, but arguments are wont to be, when they can not be found closer at hand. At the same time, truth obliges me to say, that I have a certain pleasure in it, or at least in the facts at the base of it, that it allows a view of woman and her womanly relations to man, that well accommodates our admirations, and allows us to think with great satisfaction of her future possibilities. As there is to be no marrying, or giving in marriage, so there is to be no sex, according to our common, *more humano*, sense of the terms. And yet, in the more spiritual and properly celestial sense, the two complementary natures are still on hand, and are wanted for the complete ordering and variety of the consummate social whole. Husbandhood and wifehood are there, in the old-time bonds and recollections, by which they wove their lives together, in obligations which it would be a shame even to goodness and purity ever to forget. They are married no more, and yet they are married; even as all friends are joined everlastingly to friends in the offices of truth and duty, that bound them together. In this manner the grand society of angels comprehends married people and single people, and children grouped in part according to their life-time obligations, offices, and affinities. True, there is in one view, neither male nor female there, even as the apostle declares that, in Christ, there is neither, and yet, the intolerable dryness there of a pure male state, unblessed by womanly grace and feeling, is not to be dreaded. For there is a sexhood also in spirits, as truly as in organic life, and the sex-quality is only glorified, not obliterated. But their scale of quality is, it may be, greatly changed, if not inverted in dignity. Thus the force-natures—the male—that went forward, and took the helm of government and public war, appear to have graduated now as respects their force-element, having no longer much call for either government or war upon their hands. And now come up the beauty-natures that were subject, even as Christ came up into His divine ascendency when he rose from the dead, reve ling now their quality and shining with him, "in the kingdom and patience" of his suffering Messiahship. These women, that were once put under and made subject, break into eminence now, as the soprano natures once in a while could and did in the contests of art below, and the superior fineness of their mold puts them in a tier of honor and power, which they have gloriously earned by their subject state. They were humbled, and are now exalted. Probably enough the man-spirits have more thunder in them still, but thunder is no very considerable power among the unfearing and sublimely loving good; for, to all such, quality and not quantity is the glory that most impresses their homage. And still, it may be that, as Christ, ascending out of weakness and the grave, felt "all power" gathering in upon him, in the spring of his reactions, so these women that were humbled, taking grade henceforth as angels, will the more excel in strength, and be chariots of God, more swift on their axle, when they go upon his errands.

And have we not possibly here a tolerable, or at

least, not absurd solution of that rather fine-drawn riddle by which Paul has so long plagued the commentators :—" For this cause ought the woman to have power on her head, because of the angels." The " power," that is the authority she is under, signified by her veil, ought, he argues, to be on her head, as the token of her subject womanhood, till her graduation is accomplished, and she takes her equal right among angels. She is put in this womanhood, and the subject lot of her sex, to produce a duality and the answering relationships of a twofold quality or kind—so as to spell the otherwise intolerable monotony of an isolated and single nature. Double sentiments are thus to be raised, and a beautiful dialogue of duty and feeling, in two kinds of duty, and two kinds of feeling, is to keep two echoes in play, and by so much of part and counterpart, maintain the dear society of life. This double appointment, therefore—more honorable in fact for the woman, though it does not so appear—she must never rebel against, but must wear upon her head the veil that signifies her office, till her finer nature comes to the flower. She will do it because of the angels and her own half-Christly graduation among them.

Be it then allowed, that such kind of sentiments as I am here discovering, are only put upon the Scripture, and not found in it, they are none the less worthy, and it may be, none the less true. I believe that they are from the Scripture, and reveal, as in beautiful forecast, the sublime culmination of what is called so often the dejected lot of woman. A great many things, because of the trial that is in them, are not dejected, but are only the more honorable and supremely elect. (Who in fact are the true privileged of mankind but the heroes; and who are the heroes but those who master great adversities, those who have been able to suffer, and are therefore fit to reign?) In this view it is, that I can only look with supreme pity on the campaigning women of this day, who have so far mistaken the honors of their sex, as to see no privilege but in being clear of it. They ought to see beforehand that they can not be men; and since they must be women, why should they be teaching both themselves and their sex to have a more fixed distaste of just what they must in any case be? They appear to be overmuch impressed with the clatter and clangor of our political machinery; there are so many rights in question, and such worlds of flash argument to assert them and defend them, and getting office signifies so much, and their over-easy admirations and ambitions are set in a glow, and their selfish appetite kindled puts them on asking: Why should not we go in for a part of the game also? Are we not dying for the want of something to do, and what better thing is there for us to do? Have we not as good rights as men? Have we not the same? Are we not men ourselves?

Of course they are, in some true sense of the terms, but I wish it could be seen that they think as much and have as high an opinion of being women. For one, I have a considerable satisfaction in having women; just such, I mean, as can be and love to be women. I want them exactly not to govern, not to vote, not to be the stumping power of assemblies; natures that go to make atmosphere, and not to burn it up; who can be apart, who can wait in silence, who can think it a privilege not to be required in the times of conflagration, and assume it as their finer and more gentle lot to be in the sweetness of God, and keep some flavor of it for the flavorless and hard-worn life of their husbands. They are also to be greatly desired, that they may put something into their husbands, if possible, that is fit to be enjoyed, and worthy of being respected and honored. And if they do not make history fast in this manner, God be thanked, if some are willing to live without making history. Give us women enough to do the disinterested part of the world's life, and think it all the more honorable that they do not want to be honored, and then we are so far sure that there is something great in the world. And if this be the calling of women, when they are shut away from place and power, is there any calling which they can not better afford to lose?

V.

SUBTLE MISTAKES OF FEELING AND ARGUMENT.

The false motives and mistaken arguments, that make their appearance in discussions of this subject, are too many to be recounted. To handle the whole chapter of them specifically and exhaustively is impossible, but it may be important to single out, for exposition, a few that operate most broadly and carry most effect.

It is very desirable that our women agitators in this field should understand the real motive by which they are instigated, and there is much reason to believe that they sometimes do not. There is a terrible *ennui* upon them; a want of motive, opportunity, possibility, which would even make it pardonable to break out in almost any sort of revolt, or wildest sally. They fall on the question of suffrage and political life, and get so much taken with the notion of equality propounded that, before they know it, they begin to see all the kingdoms of the world, and imagine themselves really conquering place and signification in the promised equality. It is impossible not to speak of them here with sympathy and true respect; all the greater respect, we might say, that they can dare something excessive. However heated they may be in their expectations, they are not off the basis of reason so far as to wholly misconceive the reform that engages them. The re-sexing of their sex, even so far as to make it manly in habit and action, they know to be impossible. They might very well know beside, that they will burden their condition with worse disadvantages, and heavier weights of depression, if they undertake any thing which supposes a feeling of disrespect to their sex. Probably enough they do not, but it is not difficult to see, that they are working in a kind of impatience that idealizes relief, in the subtle, undefined, indefinable, hope of some masterhood state which is somehow to be gained, in the suffrage, and to be a virtual equivalent of masculinity. Political power and place, it is believed, will mend their condition. They will conquer, in this manner, a new sphere and platform of life, where they will at least be in peerhood with men, and the dishonored, sadly depressed lot of their sex will be taken away. I believe no such thing. On the contrary, I am under a conviction, not to be resisted that the depression they are under will be greatly increased. Giving the ballot, we shall give stones for bread; putting them, as women, to a test they can not stand, and forcing them down thus into a more hopeless prostration than could otherwise ever be reached.

To say again, that I most profoundly sympathize with their endeavor, however mistaken, is unnecessary.

If I were a woman, in the present lot of women, I think I should certainly wish to be a man, and that any change, giving but a semblance of a chance that way, I should hail with delight and accept with eagerness. The wages allowed their industry are so unequal; their employments so restricted; their subjection, so often, when married, to an overbearing tyrant will they have no counter force to resist; the crime it is for them to be heart-broken, and publish their woes by the sad look of their silence; and, what is worst and saddest of all, the worse than broker's corner, wherein all unmarried women are penned by restrictions they can not escape—unable to work, because it will humble their position; unable to venture on great operations in trade, because a woman can not get the necessary credit; subject to indignities and much laughter, when they undertake a profession; wanting marriage as the proper woman's place, with a conscious ability to fill it, and with no ambition, save to be the ornament and cherished love of a worthy and true husband, yet chained fast under bonds of delicacy which well nigh forbid so much as the being approachable by a man. When, I say, these things are duly considered as pertainings of a woman's lot, we might almost justify them in a riot against natural sexhood itself, if there were any thing to be gained by it.

And yet there is one matter, just now referred to, where a genuine reform would accomplish more for women, as I verily believe, and take them out of the corner that now pinches them a great deal more certainly, than to give them a right of suffrage and of civil office; having also the farther advantage, that it would give them a more open way to the proper woman's life, for which they are made, instead of taking them off into *quasi* battles with men, for points of precedence and prerogatives of government which do not belong to them and never can; I speak here of a reform that takes off, or somehow loosens the embargo on women, as respects advances toward marriage. The assumption now is, that women must be first lassoed and taken, courted long and skillfully then and almost to the death, before they can venture an approving look. If they can not be conquered, then they must not be had, and they must take this ground themselves. On one side there must be a close fence of prudery, hard as possible to be got over; and on the other, the man who will try, must go to it bravely, which alas! for his modesty is likely to be quite impossible. Full three-quarters of the men who get stuck in their bachelor life and are never married, are in fact the most in-born adorers of women; such as never in their lives can muster courage for any advance, just because the shrine they look upon has too much divinity in it for their mortal approach. Of course it will not do for unmarried women to put themselves in a way of being suitors to men. That kind of suitorship would even be an offense, and raise a sense of revulsion; nobody would recommend to women that they get over their modesty; but the almost cholic stringency of what are called good manners, in this matter, might be relaxed, without real impropriety and with great advantage. The present iron-clad modesty, which is simply ridiculous in either party, might be so far mitigated as to let feeling feel its way, and carry on its own courtship; requiring no restriction save the restriction of words and formal advances, and allowing nature to interpret and work out her problem, hampered by no unnatural coyishness. Women can not be forward and bold, but they are now a great way further off than they need be.

There is also another way in which they are continually reducing their chances of marriage, that is far more blamable, and which certainly can be rectified; I refer to the foolish ambition they so often indulge and openly manifest, of being married into condition. There is here and there a noble-hearted young woman, such as could be willing to be joined with the small, close fortunes of a worthy, toiling man, and who would even prefer to struggle with him, and have a common title with him in his successes. But our young men are getting the impression now, and a good right to it is given them, that they can not marry till they have good condition to offer; what can they do with a wife till they have enough laid up for a wife to spend? And what is to be made of a woman, when she has no palace, and no coach, and what has she to look for but a very dull time, if she can not glitter. This very foolish ambition is due, no doubt, in a considerable degree, to the fault of the young men themselves, and the very meager and mean impression they have of women—their low, merely shop-keeper's culture, that allows them never to conceive, either a fine woman, or a true home; and yet it is largely the fault of the other sex, who suffer most by it. They themselves give it to be understood, that figure is what they expect and live for, and the hint that is so often given will about as certainly be taken. Hence again, the great diminution of marriages, and still more, of happy marriages. And the result is, that we have on hand a vast overstock of single women, dying, as it were, of *ennui*, suffocated in the feeling that they exist for nothing, and have really no place; till finally, they break out in their impatience, and resolve, at any rate, to have a place with men, as men have with each other. They are going to vote, they are going to have office; they discover, in fact, a kind of woman's millennium, in the right of woman's suffrage. Their mistake is total. It is not their present misery that they can not be men, but that they can not be women. And this latter they can be, while the former they can not. It does not appear to be seen, as yet, that government and authority are not for them, but a beginning of success will very soon bring it to light. There is not one of them all, who can settle herself to the *pose* of a judge on the bench, without being laughed at. Or, if they should get a representation in Congress, which appears to be the ambition of some, there is not cast-iron or coarse pig-metal enough in their make, to bear that kind of campaigning for any length of time. By and by, or within a ten years' time, the beautiful restraints of gallantry will be worn out, and the man-force will reduce the forlorn sisterhood to such ignominy and derision, as will finally discourage that kind of representation. If the House could scarcely abide John Randolph's treble, this chorus of treble, fluting half the time, will grow wearisome, and then annoying, and finally cease.

No; if any hopeful and true reform is possible in this matter, it must be the reform that takes off the restrictions on marriage, and facilitates the passing on of women to the true places and honors of their womanhood. And if men will not co-operate, and even be forward in that kind of reform—as it might infer some fault of delicacy in women to be—they must consent to be so far chargeable with real inhumanity. Can the Christian pulpit itself be true to its office, without applying itself, as things are now going, to the correction of our false views of marriage, and the consequently diminishing frequency of marriages? If there is a postponing on one side, instigated by a pompous and hollow ambition, utterly wide of the beautiful meaning of the family state; if on the other, where the poison of the same ambition also works, there is a consequent loss of hope and a turning away to go into fight with men in the rougher terms of equality, is it not time for the teachers of religion, the true guardians of society, to ask what duties may be now incumbent on them? And is there not, besides, a possibility of accomplishing something in this matter by organization; and so of doing more, a hundredfold, to relieve the oppressive over-stock, under which so many fine women are stifled, than will ever be done, by all the office rights and voting privileges they are now so eager to obtain. Such an organization, working only for names that are given, or by friends suggested, and presuming only, under strictest bonds of secrecy, to suggest, commend, and prepare acquaintance in ways of proper delicacy, might bridge a great many gulfs of false modesty perhaps that will otherwise be forever impassable.

In this kind of reform there is nothing unhopeful, or impossible; for it is according to nature, and not a reform against nature. The poor Buddhist women of China, for example, have abundant reason, out of their religion itself, to undertake the chance of being men, forlorn, to all appearance, as that chance may be. They were dogs, or cats, or rabbits, in the previous state, before they came hither; and the priests now ply them with a fierce, almost skinning taxation, that they may get help in securing another good transmigration in the next stage of life before them. This present state they call "the bitterness," and with very good reason; but they hope and pray, and even ache with expectation, that Buddha will give them what they call "the position of a man in good circumstances" in the future life. And if our Christian view of angels always in the masculine is correct, they might possibly get some tolerably near approach to it. But whatever woman goes after "the position of a man in good circumstances" here, is far less likely to succeed, to say the least, than she would be, if she was looking after "the position of a woman in good circumstances." This last she may get, but the other she most assuredly never will.

Now it is the very great misfortune—no, it is the glory of woman, that her position, not being either weak or low, requires so great moral refinement, a delicacy of perception so nearly celestial, to see what is really in it. The glory of it, for it is deep in glory, is that it is so unselfish.

You see this where it works instinctively, as when some really talented woman dresses up some idol of a husband, little thought of by any but herself, in the disproportionate honors and admirations of her womanly devotion; or when such a woman as the world-renowned Madame de Staël pictures her dull-witted, rather common-place father, the minister Neckar, as the great financiering genius and first statesman of his time; or when Aaron Burr's truly gifted Theodosia writes, in the almost absurd homage of her daughterhood—" You appear to me so elevated above all other men; I contemplate you with such a strange mixture of humility, admiration, reverence, love, and pride, that very little superstition would be necessary to make me worship you as a superior being, such enthusiasm does your character excite in me." These womanly homages so instinctively paid are easily and often derided as a weakness of the sex, and yet so much of worship indicates the greatness and sublimity of a worshiping nature. This feminine trust, that submerges so much of criticism, is so truly unselfish and so far away from pride, that we only the more admire its admirations. At the same time, there is, it must be allowed, a boldness and imposing prominence in the coarse, heroic airs of manly position—a noise and eclat, a bursting into admiration by force —which even a romping girl can see and be greatly taken by, or a selfish, plodding woman can easily set herself on scheming to obtain. Even as the wild, free Charlotte Elizabeth, in the boy-like rampages allowed her young nobility, was caught with desire to be a real boy, and being told that Mary Germain had transformed her sex, by jumping fairly out of it, says: "I made such terrific leaps that it was a miracle I did not break my neck." A more selfish, terribly corroding vice gets hold, not seldom, of the managing woman, which it is more sad to think of; as when it is declared of Madame de Montcalm, now sick, by her friend, the Duchess de Duras:—"She is eaten up by politics; they are her vulture." Judging from present appearances, this particular brood of vultures is getting to be largely increased.

Alas! that so many women, some of them really gifted women, should so little perceive where the honors of true womanhood lie; and that apparently, because it requires a finer degree of insight and moral sensibility than they have been able as yet to supply. They are down too nearly upon the selfish, prose level of masculine contrivings, rivalries, and struggles after power, and the poetries of their beautiful nature are too subtle and deep for their discovery. They do not conceive at all what it means to be the sex elected to gentleness and patience, or, it may be, to the dreadful lot of violence and tyrant cruelty endured; a disinterested nature, held in suppression by a hard, dry, forward, selfish nature, claiming it for husband by the homages she pays it, and hiding her really supreme glory under its coarse, forbidding masculinities. Oh! if there were nothing in this world but these workers in will and war and wrong, called men, it would be a most unblest and wretchedly dry concern. Nothing can ever lift the picture till a subject nature appears, milder, truer, and closer to the type of God's own dear submissions in the cross of his Son; allowing us to bless our sight in the beholding of so many women, by graces and benignities of self-forgetting love and sacrifice. And if still these better and elect natures want to be men, counting that an advance of condition much to be desired, God forgive us, if we quite as much want them to be women.

So much as regards the manward aspirations implied in the woman's suffrage reform. I proceed, in the next place, to speak of the very large class of inversions that overset the order of time and cause, and breed, of course, a correspondent number of sophisms. Thus it is argued, how often, that equality between man and woman is the necessary condition of affection between them; whereas it is affection rather that begets the only sense of equality. First, we have the affection based in qualities of unlikeness, that may even be called inequality, and which gives priority, managing right, and authority to the man; homages and trusts of protectorship, and upward-looking admirations, and a "seeking unto" for guardian force and "rule" on the part of the woman. Then comes equality, because the affection is so dear and complete, and so beautifully colored by the varieties of their two answering poles of character —just as the two poles of the globe compose a perfect unity because of their complementary oppositions and repugnancies. Were the two parties equal in the sense of being alike, even as two women or two men are equal, they would only be yarn, and not cloth, threads drawn parallel, but woven by no cross relations; but when the parties, a man and a woman, so unlike, are ingrafted mutually by their bisexual qualities, they are so completely one, that authority is silent, and difference almost vanishes, and it scarcely occurs to them to ask whether they are equal or not, because they are no longer two. And yet this milling of reform for women's suffrage goes on the plan of making two of the pair—either two men or two women, no matter which—and expecting, in that way of strict equality, to beget a more certain, better state of affection.

There is another inversion of true argument in this question, which is thrust upon our notice almost every day, viz., that we must have women at the polls, to civilize the polls, and be a law of grace and refinement in all public affairs. "Since the world began," says Mr. Beecher, "to refine society has been woman's function. She is

God's vicegerent on earth, for that end. You may be sure that she that has carried refinement to the household, to the church, to social life, to literature, to art, to every interest except government, will also carry it to legislation, and the whole of civil and public procedure, if it is to be carried there at all." Mr. Beecher could easily see farther if he would. Suppose it should happen to be true, that she has carried her beautiful grace into so many spheres of life and society, just because of the one exception made; viz., that she has kept herself aloof from the stormy life of intrigue, and party passion, and official command. Suppose that, being qualified by nature to be subject, and not to govern, she would even spoil the delicacy of her subject nature and become as unrefining everywhere as if she were a man. Woman is going to be acted on as well as to act, if she goes into political life; and for one, I have not much faith in what she can do by her nature when she abuses it. If the log may be split by the wooden wedge, most of us would like to be sure that the wedge is not going to be split by the log. Where away goes the refinement of the polls, when the polls have unrefined the refiner?

We encounter another inversion of order and consequent mistake of argument, in the assumption, that force or muscular superiority was the fundamental cause, at which all masculine precedence and rule began. And it is even assumed by

Mrs. J. Stuart Mill, in the *Edinburgh Review* of A. D. 1851, that a whole half of the human race, viz., the female half, are even now "passing through life in a state of forced subordination to the other half." And accordingly, it is the boast of the new women's suffrage reform, that this old reign of muscle, or masculine force, is going at last to be removed, and make room for the true equality of the sexes, and the finally complete ascendency of justice. A greater misconception will not easily be invented. The subordinate condition of women is not now a "forced subordination," and never has been to any very great extent, since the world began. The subordination is a fact universal, and never will be any less so, as long as the world continues. But it is a fact, maintained more by the natural expression of a forceful nature, than by any compelling uses of force. It is the heavy tread, and the hard-knit frame, and the thundering guttural voice, and the Jupiter-like air and expression—these it is, and man is not to blame for these—that pass the law and cast the lot of female subordination. Sometimes, especially among the savage races, it is maintained, we know, by will, and the cruel exactions of force, but it is just as truly a fact where it is never compelled by any such severities. The man-type subordinates the woman-type in all best terms of society and purest terms of morality, and will do so as long as men are men and women are women. The subordination is moral simply, based, that is, in moral expression, and no conditions of suffrage or equal count in the ballot, kept up for a dozen milleniums will take it away. It is doubtless true, as we so often hear, that women rule the world—they rule it, that is because they are subordinate; which is the most beautiful and truest rule conceivable; but that they are ever going to rule it as in chief, or by any political supremacy, is neither to be apprehended nor believed. Why, if twenty women to one man should be the relative scale of births from this time forth, the men would rule the world as completely still as ever. And they would do it too, by no exercise of force, but only by the look of it.

There is yet another kind of argument, which, instead of getting the future out of the present, gets the present out of the future. We anticipate sometimes a progress in the moral state, that will quite supersede the political, and make it possible to live, without either laws or tribunals. Having this ideal in prospect, the conclusion is sprung forthwith, that, as everybody will be doing right spontaneously, under the intrinsic sway of morality, there will of course, be no place left for " authority " in men as related to women. But suppose this fine ideal state is not yet reached, and will not be for some thousands of years, what meantime is going to settle the family council as to retisence, means of living, ways of living, and he like, when the man and the woman can not agree? The case must be decided somehow, and who shall do it? Is it the man's right, or is it the woman's? And if the man decides, taking that for his right, and even his duty, how does that decision operate? Is it a matter of force — stronger force subduing weaker—or is it simply to be a matter of right and moral conviction? I observe in all these discussions of woman's suffrage, how very nearly we Americans have lost the idea of authority. We take it as a kind of dictation-force, which is only repulsive. It is command enforced by sanctions. And that, of course, when taken as the authority of man, is simply odious; whereas all true authority operates in and through moral convictions only. "This man speaks with authority," said the people, "not as the scribes." They did not mean that Christ was uttering law and maintaining it by force, but they meant that his sentiments and his personal air affirmed themselves, and carried conviction by their own pure emphasis. This was his authority. There was, it is true, a kind of authority in him that went with force, as when he drove the profane hucksters out of the temple; and yet the remarkable thing even there was, that he carried nothing by the application of his rods, but every thing by the sacredly impressive heat of his indignations. In short, no conception is really more unworthy and low than that which resolves authority into force, and even

THE REFORM AGAINST NATURE. 105

imagines that the moral progress of society—which is, in fact, to culminate in the completely sovereign authority of moral ideas—will therefore take it quite away.

We pass now to another class of mistaken arguments and false assumptions, that grow out of some comparative estimate of the sexes, which is too hasty and crude to support any rational conclusion. Thus it is maintained that woman is not in any sense more complementary to man than man to woman. And it is doubtless true, that woman is to be more complete in womanhood because of man, even as man is to be more complete in manhood because of woman. But it does not follow that she represents humanity in the same way, and has an equal right to do it by the same things. That has never been the sense of the world. In all known languages, we call the human race *man*, and never call it *woman*. And when we speak in this manner, we do it in the feeling that every particular man and woman has a complementary office to fill under the generic word *man*, which complementary office every particular man fills in a sense more primary and capital, and every woman in a sense more secondary and subordinate. Paul words the relation just as we do, and just as we see it with our eyes—"neither was the man created for the woman, but the woman for the man."

Again, it is affirmed, with perfect truth, that

woman has just as good right as man to assert and improve her own individuality; whereupon the sophistry comes in by an inference, that she has just as good right as he to vote, and have office, and be a campaigner with men in their political strifes and ambitions. Suppose it should happen to be true, that going into that particular field is against all perfection of her individuality, that her womanly qualities are too delicately fine, too close to the pure intuitions of morality, to suffer any thing but damage in such rough ways of encounter; what in that case becomes of the argument? Instead of showing that she has just as good right as men to be banged, and battered, and go a wrestling; it shows that her beautiful womanly individuality demands a softer element, and a more sheltered way of life, where she may get as much authority of another kind and a sovereignty as much more complete as it will be more undisputed. And what, if then, it should be proved, that men have no more right of authority over women than women over men? Yet the kind of authority the woman is to get, and was really made for, is how different—so different that if she were to go a stumping for it, hoping to win it by the sublime rage of a candidacy, she would come out *minus*, even in her victory, to be no authority at all. The precise way for women never to gain, always to miss their kind of authority, is to go after the other kind at the polls.

Again, it is argued that, as culture reduces the distinctness of the sexes, we are to presume a final obliteration of their distinguishing qualities, and turn both sexes into the great field of public action together. I must totally deny both the assumption and the inference made from it. Not even Mr. Darwin, as far as I know, expects to get the races, any of them, clear of sex, and pass them finally by it. He finds no principle of natural selection, that is going to select only males, or only females. Meantime, the conception that the sexes are approximated by culture is too superficial to bear inspection. Perfect the English taste and style of a man and the English taste and style of a woman, and how plausible in appearance will the assimilation be; and yet they will appear, on close inspection, to be only more wonderfully male and female. Put them into the absolute science of geometry, and they will somehow make you feel as if one were engineering a camp, and the other a lace or a stocking. Give them both such complete training, that they will both be respected equally for their good sense, and then it will come up as the deepest kind of riddle, that two very sensible people can be so different. Bring them into the very same ways of thinking, and then it will be discovered that the same ways of thinking do not, after all, make the man-mind and the woman-mind work alike, but a great way from it. The reason why we assume that culture approximates the characters of men and women is, that we merely note first points of resemblance; whereas, if we attend more closely, and penetrate the question more perceptively, we have all our impressions reversed. And it ought to be so, as we might well enough see beforehand. Is it not plain, even to our eyes, that the man-quality and the woman-quality are unlike? How then is the mere development of these qualities going to make them alike? What can such development do but just bring out the unlike qualities? And what is that but to make them more unlike?

Once more—it is often assumed that the sexes are designed to create character in each other; therefore, that women require to be raised in the manly parts and functions, in order to the true raising of men. And the writer above referred to in the *Edinburgh Review* goes so far as to say that, "In the present close association between the sexes, men can not retain manliness unless women acquire it." But we have had some rather manly men in the past ages of the world, and we have perhaps a rather larger proportion, even now. And yet we do not find that many of our women are quite willing as yet, to set up for being manly women. Besides, if the assimilating power works both ways in the manner stated, how are the women ever to become more womanly unless the men become womanly enough to help them? And here the whole masculine nature, nay, and the whole female nature to boot, are out together in stern protest that men shall be men, and not women at all. Every woman wants a man for her husband, and every husband wants to be a man. The argument therefore breaks down utterly; manly women are not wanted, and womanly men are not wanted, and most happy it is, in both cases, that they are not; for it is opposites here, and not similarities, that make the power. The man will be manlier, that he has a true womanly wife, and the wife will be the more womanly, that she has a manly husband. Develop both natures to the utmost, and the development of each will help that of the other. Nothing is more utterly preposterous, and more totally contrary to fact, than that, if we are to have manlier men, we must put the women out into fight, and bronze their soft faces into unbearded manliness at the tug of the polls. Why, if we could get the poor women up to this necessary pitch of manliness, and make them stalwart and bold as Lucifer, is there no reason to fear that, on principles of natural selection, we might prefer to let them have the polls and migrate to some more congenial country.

VI.

THE REPORT OF HISTORY.

Women's suffrage is not a fact of history, but is rather a fact on the outside of history, waiting to get in. We have known but a single example of it; which continued scarcely long enough to be any example at all. I refer of course to the brief chapter furnished us by the State of New Jersey. The Constitution of '76 allowed " all inhabitants of full age, and worth fifty pounds," the elective franchise. Fourteen years after, viz: in 1790, the Legislature, in revising the statute, consented, at the instance of a Quaker gentleman, to take off the ambiguity some had felt as regards the meaning of the Constitution, by inserting the words " he or she." Seven years afterward, that is, in 1797, the amended statute was farther amended, by inserting the word "*free.*" As yet, during the space of twenty-one years, there had been no instance of female voting, but the contest raging now between the old Federal and Democratic parties, brought up two candidates for the Council that stood in close balance, and the committee on one side, just before the polls were closed for the day, offered, quite unexpectedly, a number of female voters—the *Newark Centinel* said seventy-five—who could not of course be rejected. Three years later in the Presidential canvass of 1800, when Adams and Jefferson were the candidates, the women voted almost universally throughout the State —women of all colors—from the age of 18 upward. Two years later, in 1802, at a contested election the votes of two or three colored women determined the choice of a representative. This fact excited some dissatisfaction, but nothing was done to obtain a repeal of the law, till after another election, by which it was to be tested yet more severely. The question of the county seat, that is of the location of the court house and jail for Essex County, was the point now in issue, and the trial lay between Newark and Elizabethtown. The excitement of the contest ran high, and nothing was omitted, right or wrong, probably, that could help to carry the vote. The women of all colors and ages swore to their estate of fifty pounds, and insisting on their constitutional right, would not be excluded; for what board of inspectors could be rough enough to exclude the suffrage right of women? And the voting, it seems, grew livelier all day, for as Mr. Whitehead informs us, the women voted "not only once, but as often, as by change of dress,"—who can manage that like a woman? and where is the end of it !—" or complicity of the inspectors, they might be able to repeat the process."

The result was that the Legislature, at their next session, thoroughly disgusted by the palpable frauds of the canvass, set aside the vote by their own act, and located the county seat themselves.

Now, it will be said, I suppose, that this was but a rude, unregulated trial, where the precedents had not gathered body enough, as yet, to govern the proceedings. And yet there had been a voting by women eleven years ago, and a general voting by all the women of the State six years ago. At any rate, we have in this brief chapter of experiment, a really appalling refutation of the promise so frequently made in these discussions, that when women come to the vote, they will bring in honesty and decency, and make a full end of the frauds we now deplore and think of with so great alarm. On the contrary we see, as distinctly as need be, that women, never trained to consider what is in a vote, may have the lightest possible conception of it, and can be if they will, the corruptest, most unmanageable voters in the world. Besides, we can also see as distinctly that no board of Inspectors will ever be able to detect the disguises that women can put on, by assuming many varieties of dress. They have every facility in the matter of dress, for taking on fifty characters in a day, and voting them all, without any least probability of detection.

Accordingly, when the Legislature of New Jersey, in the very next year, A. D. 1807, come to the conclusion, that they have had enough of women's suffrage and will now be clear of it—when they take up their parable and begin to say, " Whereas it is highly necessary to safety, quiet, good order, and dignity of the State," &c., &c., it is rather difficult not to be imagining what we all, in every State, shall want to say after a like experiment. Shall we be able to say it, or will it be too late?

There is no other example, so far as I know, that can be cited for this point, unless it be that women have been allowed both to vote and to speak in our Baptist and Methodist churches, and sometimes, lately, in our Congregational churches—also that they are set in offices of administration, and sometimes even put in a kind of apostleship, by the Christian assemblies of the Quakers. But here, of course, no such bad consequences of the suffrage follow, for the very manifest reason, that whatever is done by the women is done as in a liberty of prophesying. They do not propose to act from themselves, or for themselves, as when they measure themselves with men at the polls, but to act as in the spirit and as vehicles of a divine grace and teaching. This very wide distinction sufficiently conserves their modesty, and it must be confessed that in the case of the Quakers, it appears to sufficiently conserve their modesty also in the use of their administrative functions, where it could not as well be expected.

Dropping now these more particular illustra-

tions where some kind of voting has been allowed
to women, I propose another and more general
kind of argument, which, including many modes
and varieties, may be expected to justify itself as it
proceeds. The general verdict of history, as I
conceive, is something like this, that some kind of
mischief, or bad fatality has been almost always
discoverable, where women have become forward
actors and managers in political affairs.

This I know is not the common impression.
What in fact do we hear, several times a day, when
it is alleged that women have no governing right
and no fitness to be in places of authority, but that
England, one of the greatest and most forward
kingdoms of the world, has a queen for its ruler,
a woman celebrated for no specially brilliant gifts,
and yet a much respected, properly successful head
magistrate. If now this particular English woman
can rule one empire, may not other women often
more gifted, suffice to make good voters, or even
good under-magistrates? But if we are to come at
the real merit of this argument, it may be very important to find, when the queen bears rule, who
rules the queen? No woman stands higher probably in the scale of ability to govern, than the famous Isabella of Spain. And yet, if we will see
the exact truth, she is nothing but a lay-figure
queen, behind whom stands her great high councilor Ximenes, robing her with honors from himself.
She, that is Ximenes, hedged about her husband

as by a kind of sentry guard, fortified him by ceremonies, tied him up by oaths, all which may have been very kind, but not particularly gracious. She also, that is Ximenes, prepared the Inquisition by his priestly counsel, leaving it to her to adorn his red dragon institute by her beautiful graces and charms. There was nothing in fact that could be called a felicity in her administration, but the ornament she could put in oppression, and fettering, unreliable aid she gave to Columbus. Take away Ximenes, and there is no counsel; take away Columbus, and there is no brightening fact or glory.

There is also another consideration, as respects these reigning women. After all, they are not women, but men; for they do not stand in their lines as successors of women, but in almost all cases as successors of men. The gap they fill is a gap in some male line. And they bring very little into it commonly but their name and signature. They are like ciphers between the other figures, important for the spacing they make, and not for what they signify themselves. They sign as women, rule as women, it is true, but the function they wield is felt, both by themselves and their people, to be a man's function, and the queenhood of it has a certain masculine force, because it is only a bridge that connects a future with a former masculine order and law. Besides, the councilors and chief ministers are always men, and there is not, in fact, a queen of all Europe and probably never was, who could make a woman her chief minister, and carry on the government. Kings enough there have been, that were managed and kept by women, when proposing to have men for their council; but no queen could hold her place a week, having only feminine statesmen for her ministers. In all which we perceive, as clearly as need be, that the queenly governments are after all rather masculine than feminine.

Take now a single other example in this field, and it shall be the one that favors least the view just presented; the example I mean of Elizabeth of England. She came to the throne, not as succeeding a man, but a woman, which so far was a considerable disadvantage; and yet, when viewed more closely, it will be seen to have put her in a condition of the greatest possible advantage. For Mary, who came in after Edward, had been a great disappointment and affliction to all best feeling in the nation, so that when Elizabeth came in, after Mary, she was hailed with great eagerness and expectation, as the true successor of Edward. In this manner she derived no small part of her prestige in the government, from the fact that she represented the Protestant cause in such manner as could be expected of no other princely character of the time.

And what now shall we say of her reign? Superficially regarded, or surveyed from a little distance off, it appears to be thoroughly successful, and historians have written most admiringly of the splendid ability displayed by her queenly administration. But if we are disposed to have a deeper inspection of her merit, we find it very nearly impossible to imagine, that a woman of so many weaknesses, and tossed by so many uncomfortable tempers, can have added much to the success of her reign that was fairly from herself. She was surrounded, as it were, and caged by a body of nobles, and grave councilors, and great men pillared in wise moderation and heroic self-respect, and she knocked herself about among them, first against one, and then against another, persecuting some, annoying all, and calling it government; whereas, in fact, they all were governing her with as much patience as they could, or as much impatience as they must, and keeping her, by their changing attractions and repulsions, within the endurable conditions. There was never a finer illustration of the fact that women as such are not called to use authority, for with all the force she employed, the tyrannical edicts she pronounced, and the imperious and haughty airs she assumed, she was held up largely by the courteously moderated pity of her great men; and as to genuine personal authority, she had never a trace of it in the feeling of anybody. She had an almost universal jealousy of women, and especially of fine women. Indeed she very nearly hated the sex, passing her order in a progress through Essex and Sussex, "that no head or member of any college, or cathedral, should bring a wife, or any other woman, into the precincts of it to abide in the same, on pain of forfeiture of all ecclesiastical promotion." In her style, we discover an almost laughable ambition to show herself a man; rolling on her ponderous convolutions of dignity in the unimpressive tumble of a school of porpoises at sea, all the while about to say something manly in a manly way, only finding at last no place for it. She is courted by everybody, and wants to be courted by twice as many. She promises her people that she will marry, but is kept from it apparently, by the unwelcome fact that her husband will be the last of her suitors. She receives whole cargoes of *billet-doux* in the most laughable and absurd excesses of flattery, all of which she is fool enough to value, and store away for the future, instead of throwing them in the fire—else why are they now preserved to us? She was not less sure that her vixenly face was beautiful, than she was that she was doing every thing in the kingdom herself. She, Elizabeth, supported the French Huguenots; she, Elizabeth, took the part of the Low Countries; she, Elizabeth, vanquished the Spanish armada; she, Elizabeth, was, in fact, the general doer of all that went on. No; there was one thing she did not do—the death of Mary, Queen of Scots—she wept over that!

Now it is not to be denied that England was brought on a great way, in the long reign of Elizabeth. Things were at a certain renovation-point, where they must go on somehow unless very much hindered, and forty-five years of duration must show a considerable stride of advance if they showed any. Her court endured her as an odious, royally detestable woman, and sought to make the best of her as far as they could. And when she died it was not a day too soon. She had filled the masculine gap, and been as much of a man in the line, as perhaps she could; but they wanted now a man—whether to be worse or better, they must learn for themselves. Perhaps it may be said with truth, as it is in fact often said, that Elizabeth of England is the highest example of queenly authority afforded by the history of the world. I have sketched this outline of her reign, partly in deference to that impression; and it is under the same, that we so often have the argument for woman's suffrage and her right of rule, turned by the citation of her example. But she was only a bad core in a fair apple; and if another woman had succeeded her, promising to be just like her in her rule, it is doubtful whether she could have held the reins in hand for a single six-months.

I have spent thus much of time on the governing women, because they are cited with so great frequency and confidence in the general question

I am discussing. In the first place, they are in men's places just to personate the filling of them, and be helped by the male formalities of the position. In the next place, they do every thing by men, and so, putting always the very highest male talent of the nation at the point of real headship over its affairs. And then, once more, they have never in any one case, shown more than a very meager authority and capacity of rule in themselves.

Taking now a more decisive and direct way of argument, let us look along down the lines of history and see how far the part women have taken in government, and their very close association with government, and with governing men, has operated well or beneficently. We have two examples in history, one ancient and the other modern, where women have taken the military command, by a purely divine call, and have, so far, administered a sovereignty in God's name, independently of all human control. I speak of Deborah the prophetess and Joan of Arc. They are unlike in some respects, and more unlike, if we take the sublime lyric of Deborah as written by herself, and not as composed for her by some admiring poet who had caught the inspirations of her story. But they both agree in this, that they act, not in their own will and council, but by a certain irruption of divine impulse upon them. They do not so much fight in a way of moving battle, as sail over their fields, and see the hand of God working for them. They are God's angels now, before their time, set on like David's twenty thousand angels who are twenty thousand chariots of God. It is not important to settle the precise function by which they operate, or how far they may be raised ecstatically above or out of themselves. Enough that they are prophetesses in some very superlative sense, and are therefore not examples to be cited, in a question that is only concerned to find what capacities of public life and rule belong to women, as acting from their natural functions. The talk of Balaam's animal might as well be cited to show the talking capacity of his kind. With these two wonderful women some class Judith, and perhaps rightly, only she appears to be rather fanatically possessed than ecstatically raised, in the bloody feat of her story.

Opening a little more largely now the scripture history, we discover as many as five pairs of characters that exhibit, in one light or another, the agency of women, acting through, or upon the governing power in their husbands. The best, and only satisfactory one of the five, is revealed in the story of Esther and Ahasuerus. Here we have a good illustration of what power there may be in beauty, or the subject state of beauty, as compared with force. An exquisitely fascinating woman, as beautiful in her manners and character, it would seem, as in her person, yet the daughter of a captive and generally despised race, has such power with a haughty monarch, that she is able, by her intercession, to turn the resentments of his proud ministers upon their own head, and also to deliver her despised race from an edict of extermination already proclaimed. She governs in a sense the government, and yet without exercising or exhibiting, any one political or governing talent in herself. She is manipulated in her story, at every turn, by her brave uncle Mordecai; and apart from him, she is only a simple Jewish girl. He it is that makes her what she is, and does by her what she does.

The case of Pilate's wife and Pilate is different, but scarcely less interesting. Who she was we do not know, but she probably was young, and had not been hardened as yet by the false casuistries of public life. She is simple, unsophisticated, has the tender and true feeling—all that is included in the morally perceptive insight of a woman; being the only one of all the unbelieving crowd on that dreadful day of the trial of Jesus, who distinctly saw his innocence, and felt her womanly sympathies drawn out for him. She was perhaps a Jewess and religious, for she had dreams that took hold of her religious nature, and filled her with dread of some unknown evil impending over her husband and the nation. Her warning evidently shook him, but it did not quite prevail. Here is a woman at the side of the government, it must be confessed, who sees farther into the great matter in question than all the priests and magistrates, and who, if the decision had been hers, would have brought the trial to a different issue. And yet, if she had been the magistrate presiding, she could not have controlled the crowd, or maintained even a semblance of order, and the close would have been a murder by the mob not less revolting. A great many women would seize more unerringly on the judicial merit of accused persons, than even the most competent judges, and yet having no gift of authority, they could not steady the order of proceedings sufficiently to save the tribunal of justice itself.

A third of the cases referred to is furnished by Samson; a man raised up for government, who yet is taken away from his very calling itself, and made a cipher, by his subjection to a woman. No other character in all human history, excepting Christ himself, begins upon as high a key of prospect, as this very absurd man Samson. Supernaturally promised, in signs of surpassing sublimity; nourished in the strictest and most sacred terms of virtue; gifted alike with prowess, and strength, and wit, and poetry; raised up, we should say, to be the deliverer of his people, in their wretched state of anarchy and defeat; he yet justifies no expectation, lives to no purpose, and goes out finally, as a snuffed candle, at the end of a most foolish and absurd life. And the secret of his wretched collapse is, that he is caught in the coils of an artful and intriguing wife, who is too good a Philistine to let him be a Jew, and is only going to make him show how a great strong man and predestined champion, may be taken away from his country and his time and the expectation of his time, by a fascinating and perfidious woman.

Ahab was a much less promising character than Samson to begin with, and it may be that Jezebel did not make him a great deal worse. But she did what she could, and by her devilish instigation, would have made a much better king the insufferable tyrant and robber of his people.

What kind of influence Herodias had upon Herod, we know; and the probability is, that this bad woman had been training in his brother Philip's court, for just such kind of monstrosities—the taking off of a good man's head, the head of a prophet, that she might spite his faithfulness, and turn his reproofs to mockery. It was no advantage certainly, to Herod, that he had this helper by him in his government.

Turning now to the Greek and Roman histories, I will cite the instance of the two most forward public women in both: viz., Aspasia and Cleopatra. We do not as definitely know the story of Aspasia as we could wish. She is sometimes reported in terms, that put her at a low point in the scale of virtue. Pericles was undoubtedly captivated by her charms, as he might very well be, and he may have divorced his own wife to put himself more completely in her power. She could not have been a loose or low woman. There appears, in fact, to be no better example in all history, of what a woman near the state may have the talent to accomplish, than hers. But her mode of life does not indicate that she was a political or managing woman. She was a woman rather of society, and moved on the state principally by the great inspirations she excited. The story that she wrote one of the chief orations of Pericles was probably not true, but she may have given him all needed thoughts and inspirations for it. That she raised two public wars, is not much believed; though she may have put some fire into the wars after they were kindled. She kept her house open, maintaining a kind of general levee for the principal men and women of the city; in doing which, she was not so much garnishing the court of Pericles, as he himself providing the honors of the court of Aspasia. The fascinations of her beauty, and the still more fascinating charms of her conversations, made her the adored woman, and her house the shrine of all the great men of Athens. Here it was that oratory and style in writing found their true ideal and true laws of criticism. Here came up all the great questions of art; for it was the birthday of art for the city. Phidias the sculptor, Damon the musician, Euripides the king of tragedy—all these and others, caught their fires and took their ideals here. Plato came in often, and did not omit, on a cer-

tain occasion, to congratulate her and the city on
the speech she had made over the fallen at the
battle of Lechæum. Socrates himself confesses
the great benefit he has received from this wonderful woman. After the death of Pericles, discovering something hopeful in one Lysicles, an
obscure person, she set the tide of her inspirations
lifting under him, and made even him a respected,
widely influential citizen. She quickened, as it
were, the whole mind of her time, and was felt as
a soul of beauty going through every department of Athenian life and society. All which, it
will be claimed by some, makes her a striking example of what a woman may do in the spheres of
public office and power. On the contrary, it could
not be more visible, it seems to me, that had she
been a managing woman at all, she never could
have been any thing else that she was. She
swayed the state, she filled the city with ornament
and life, flowing down, as it were, upon all art and
society from above. And in this view, she is even
a most clear example of how much might be spoil-
ed in a great woman, by getting her submerged
under the stresses and managing devices of what
is called statesmanship. Done up in state-craft;
Aspasia would have only been a very common
woman, and not in any sense the quickening soul
of her times.

Cleopatra figures in the Roman story after a
fashion equally conspicuous, but in ways of politi-

cal intrigue that are only ways of mischief. She loses a throne, and she gains it two or three times over, by the fascinations of her beauty and the unmatched elegance of her manners. Now she governs with a Cæsar, and now she undertakes for Antony, feasting with him till they both have wasted their opportunities, and then fighting a battle at sea for him, to lose it by mere panic and die with him in the fatalities of a common disgrace. And yet her fatalities are only the fatalities of an immensely talented and almost oversplendid woman. She played her sex into the stake, as what woman is not likely to do, and the passion of the mixture took away the discretion, making public affairs the pretext only of her private heats and follies.

Pass on now to a large, long chapter, full of instruction as regards this question of the true womanly place in government, the chapter I mean which comprises the history of so many Louises, on the downhill slope of the kingdom: viz., the four that preceded the Revolution. Nothing distinguishes these 150 years of history so completely, as to say that they are the times of the mistresses. The kings governed the kingdom, and the mistresses governed the kings. And the mistresses commenced, tier above tier, and tier behind tier, pushing on their rivalries and their infinite cross combinations, stopping short of murder, when it was convenient, not otherwise, caring nothing for the state, save to make it yield what money may be wanted, frittering away and rotting down all public love, and making all high character a prey. There was no morality, or truth, or public love. The intercourse of palaces was the intercourse of lies. The womanly state-craft everybody knew was heartless, cruel; instigated only by hate and jealousy, and all base passion. Nobody believed any thing, and there was nothing to be believed. The kings cared nothing for their people, wanted nothing but to please their women, and keep up the necessary appearances. In this terrible loathsomeness, the core of the nation was rotting for so long a time; till, finally, there was not fiber enough left to hold the functions of the state together; and who was governing, at any given time, this woman or that, or the king, or the king's chief minister, no one knew. Sometimes not even the royal council could tell what hand was moving in this or that affair. Thus, poor Neckar, the minister, not consulted when M. Antoinette was gathering the military to put down the States General, says: "I never knew, with any degree of certainty, the end at which the queen's party wished to arrive. There were secrets, and secrets within secrets, and I believe that the king himself was not acquainted with them all. It was probably determined, as circumstances afforded opportunity, to inveigle the king into measures no one would have ventured to mention to him directly." Next-day

Neckar was dismissed and sent into exile, and as good room and space were given for the pending revolution as need be. After 150 years of state-mistressing, after so many cabals of the woman cabinets, and such immense concoctions of "secrets within secrets" which composed their statecraft, government was in fact already worn out and gone, ended before the revolution, and the revolution came in fact just because it was ended. The *finis* was already reached, and nothing remained but to shut up the book and put it away.

Now these rapid and rather desultory glances at what may be called the governing agencies of women reveal, as the general fact, a great want of felicity in them. They have done best when filling occasional gaps in the male succession of thrones, and worst, by a great deal, when mixed with men, to reign as favorites and be themselves the wisdom of courts. Taken as councilors, dispensers of offices and honors, first managers and specially skilled intriguers, they have made a very disorderly and mean history. When we put them to the ballot, and give them rights of office, their relations to men will be different; far less select, and probably, after a short time, quite as deep in the intrigues both of sex and office together. Indeed, we can not comprehend at all this matter of women's suffrage till we make distinct account of the joint working of these two kinds of intrigues.

We can possibly bear the intrigues of men, for they have but a single character; but what can we do when the double complications of two such double-acting intrigues are twisted into the web of our society and public policy and public law? If it does not shortly become the foulest mixture the world has seen, it will not be that all necessary ingredients and opportunities are wanting. This harnessing of men and women together, and calling it government, is making, in fact, a conjunction against nature, which has the doom of failure on it beforehand. The great law commentator, Montesquieu, says, that "women have naturally so many duties to fulfill, duties which are peculiarly theirs, that they can not be sufficiently excluded from every thing inspiring other ideas." I would say, instead, that government is to govern, and that women are not; and therefore, that when government makes conjunction with women, it must take up ideas that can not be sufficiently excluded.

It is a common assumption that appears and reappears at every turn in the advocacy of women's suffrage, that our elections will be moderated and made more respectable by the presence and participation of women; because the women themselves will be more restrained in their manners, and will have a restraining, mitigating effect on the men. Nothing could be more agreeable to be hoped, and when we note the civilizing effect of the presence of women, coming in as they sometimes do, to grace our public assemblies, we are tempted to believe that such kind of advantages will be gained. But we need not go far, I think, to gather up facts or incidents that indicate a result exactly opposite. Women admire a great deal more strongly than men, and when they have a candidate, one who has become the idol of their choice, there is nothing they will not do to carry their end in his election; just as the proud Duchess of Devonshire allowed a butcher at the hustings to kiss her, on condition of his voting for Fox. If this high-life, conventional woman could be so far taken out of the proprieties, in the hope of gaining a vote, how will it be with all sorts of women, mixing with all sorts of men, in-doors and out-of-doors, and playing such intrigues of candidacy, for weeks before and after, as the candidates of both sexes can arrange in the farming of their vote. For a time, for three or four elections probably, the effect may be only good, but no such conjunction of men and women, in the fierce struggles and heats of party, can ever be kept on foot for any length of time, without breeding results of profligacy that are fearfully disastrous.

At the same time it is not true that women take excitements less severely than men. We think so now, because we have them at such a remove of distance as allows them to be kept in softer tempers. But what have we seen at the South, but that women are the most intolerant, most unreasoning haters to be found. We may almost say that it was the women, goading the men, who finally forced them into rebellion. And what do we see but that women even now, as in Texas, are determined to have their animosity, and, at least, to get the satisfaction of having duly punished somebody. And the picture they are in is only the more absurd, that they keep their hate alive, when there is no longer anybody alive to feel it. In all which we are to see that women are the most violent partisans in the world, and that nothing is more certain, when the women's suffrage plan is carried, than that all party contests will be raised to a pitch of exasperation never before seen. We ought to anticipate just this from what we know of men themselves; for there is a certain class of men that have a softer fiber, and a finer and more fragile person, and these are always the persons to be most extravagant, most violent, and most fiercely denunciatory in all measures and causes of reform. The sturdy, thick-bodied, masculine men keep their balance and their key of moderation, but these others are vitriol and gall to every sort of opposition. Accordingly we shall see, when the days of women's suffrage are come, that all we had to say of moderation and a gentler type of manners, in our political affairs, has been a most sad mistake, that party strife was never before so bitter and so mixed with hate. Women are a great deal more violent, constitutionally speaking, than men;

the very delicacy of their nature makes them so, and as soon as they are called to violence, which now they are not, they will make an element of unmitigated bitterness. When the charities of a womanly nature are burned out, and nothing left but spleen or frenzied passion, we have a spectacle both sad and frightful.

VII.

PROBABLE EFFECTS.

I alluded just now, in the close of the last chapter, to one or two facts in which we get slight indications of the pitch of excitement to which women are likely to be carried in the field of political action, and also of the kinds and qualities of that excitement; how far loosened from the womanly proprieties, how fierce possibly, and bitter it may be. We have only a very few facts developed as yet, to show how this almost unknown type of progress, so called, is going to behave itself. Many persons never see any thing by their imagination, taking it for granted, that what is fact, is going to be fact, and that under all newest, most untried conditions, fact will behave just as it always has. In this way it is taken for granted, we may see, in the most innocent way possible, that women are going to be women as they always have been; to be gentle, retired, quiet, unselfish, carrying an element of dignity, and grace, and presiding good manners into the caucuses and campaign assemblies of which they are become a part; just as they did when they came in, once in four or five years, to fill a gallery and look on. And so it is computed that when they drop into place under the new reform, to be political women, they will inaugurate a kind of millennial age of good manners and respectful conduct, by which every thing in political life and society will be raised. Such kind of prognostications are simply stupid, wholly without perception. Why the change we are proposing here is radical enough, when time enough is added, to alter even the type of womanhood itself. At first, or for a short time, the effect will not be so remarkable, but in five years, and still more impressively in twenty-five, it will be showing what kind of power is in it. And if still it should go on for some hundreds of years, as it is of course expected that it will, it will become a fact organic and constituent in the race, and the very look and temperament of women will be altered. The word *woman* of course will remain to denote the female sex of man, but the personal habit and type of the sex will be no more what it is. The look will be sharp, the voice will be wiry and shrill, the action will be angular and abrupt, wiliness, self-asserting boldness, eagerness for place and power will get into the expression more and more distinctly, and become inbred in the native habit. Hitherto we have been calling the female sex the fair sex, and that word *fair* represents, in bloom and beauty, just what the elect virtues of womanhood—the trust, the unselfishness, the deep kindliness, the ethereal grace and cheer, the facile and free-playing inspirations —call for as their fit expression. Accordingly, when these softer virtues go by, giving way to the ambitions of candidacy, and the subtle intrigues of party, they will carry off with them the fair colors, the flushes of clean sensibility, and the delicate, smooth lines of form and feature, and we shall have, instead, a race of forward, selfish, politician-women coming out in their resulting type, thin, hungry-looking, cream-tartar faces, bearing a sharper look of talent, yet somehow touched with blight and fallen out of luster. If it could be expected, that as they change type physiologically, they will become taller and more brawny, and get bigger hands and feet, and a heavier weight of brain, it would not be so much to their disadvantage, and perhaps there will be some little approach to compensation in this way, but there is far more reason to fear that the fight they are to be in, being a fight against nature, will make them at the same time thinner, sharp-featured, lank and dry, just as all disappointed, over-instigated natures always are.

I speak thus of the physiological changes, or changes of type, that are going to be wrought in womanhood, not because it is a matter of principal concern with me, that women should keep their beauty, but simply that, by these external, physiological tokens, I may raise a more adequate conception of the immense moral transformation that is going to be wrought in their personal temperament and character. Nevertheless, it is a truth most deeply grounded, that women are bound, in God's name, to save their beauty. For this is the honor and power of their subject state. Man rules by the precedence of quantity and self-asserting energy, and woman by the subject sovereignty of beauty, personal and moral together, which she can little afford to lose by a sally to gain the noisier, coarser kind that does not belong to her—which also she will as certainly fail of, as the governing of men she is after, is both against their nature and her own.

Be this as it may, it will be a very great oversight in us not to perceive that this introduction of women to an active part in political affairs will be followed by an immense change in the womanly habit and character, and a change about equally undesirable to both sexes. The new possibility will at first be a triumph for women, and will seem to be the dawn of a higher and more hopeful state; but in the long run of time the change will be the running down of womanhood into weakness and contempt. The beautiful prestige now held will be gone, her fatal want of faculty to cope with men in public affairs will be proved, and she will be irrevocably battered and draggled by the kind of encounter in which she has so miserably failed. And it will be a failure all the worse, and more hopeless, that it will have burnt away so many fine properties and lost her the standing she had, by God's appointment, in her nature itself. Her successes will be short and partial, and when the present stock of gallantry is expended, instead of being helped and put forward because she is a woman, she will rather be hindered, because, being a woman, she can be. Coming thus to the end, where favor dies, she is neither the elect nor the elected lady longer, and no matter what her worth may be, it will be strange if she does not suffer a good deal of moral damage in her collapse.

The active, campaigning work of political life is certainly in quite too high a key for the delicate organization, and the fearfully excitable susceptibilities of women. They have no conception now, as they look on, of the gustiness and high tempest their frail skiffs must encounter. The struggle is a trial even for men, that sometimes quite overturns their self-mastery, and totally breaks down the strength both of their principles and their bodies. And yet if we enlarge the contest, as we must, when we bring in women, it will be manifold more intense than now. Hitherto it has been an advantage to be going into battle in our suffrages with a full half, and that the best half morally, as a corps of reserve, left behind, so that we may fall back on this quiet element or base, several times a day, and always at night, and recompose our courage and settle again our mental and moral equilibrium. Now it is proposed that we have no reserve any longer, that we go into our conflicts taking our women with us, all to be kept heating in the same fire for weeks or months together, without interspacings of rest, or cooling times of composure. We are to be as much more excited, of course, in this new dispensation as we can be, and the women are of course to be as much more excited than we, as they are more excitable. Let no man imagine, as we see to be the way of many, that our women are going into these encounters to be just as quiet, or as little moved as now, when they stay in the rear unexcited, letting us come back to them often and recover our reason. They are no more mitigators now, but instigators rather, sweltering in the same fierce heats and commotions, only more tempestuously stirred than we. What we take by first hand impulse they take by exaggeration. And accordingly, it will be seen that, where we are simply at red heat, they are at white; that where we deprecate, they hate; that where we touch the limits of reason, they touch the limits of excess; that where we are impetuous in a cause, they are uncontrolable in it. We knew how as men to be moderated in part, by self-moderation, even as ships, by their helms, in all great storms at sea; for the other part, we had women kept in moderation by their element, even as ships in harbor lie swinging by their anchors; but now, we get even less of help from these than they do from us. I do not mean by this that women do not show as brave self-keeping often as men, but that going more by feeling than men, they feel every thing more intensely, and with more liabilities to excess. They make more of their idols, too, than men do, raise more false halos about them, and even have it as a kind of virtue to bear defeat badly in their cause. Hard pushed by adversaries, they almost certainly count them personal enemies. It is not that some hysterical, over-delicate women are prone to such exaggerations of sensibility, but that, like our southern women, or the tough city mothers of Sparta, they too commonly allow their passions to get heated, and call it their righteous sentiment. To conceive our whole popular mass, both male and female, seething, at once, in the same vortex of party commotion—ten women taking hold of one man to at once possess and dispossess him in their higher key of excitement—is no pleasant thing to contemplate. But the specially sad thing of it is, not that men will be heated and put to a strain and made coarse, possibly violent, but that women will be. Men are made to be coarse after a certain masculine fashion, but there is no such masculine fashion for women. But whether there be or not, fifty years in such kind of training will even transform the womanly temperament. Will it not, as certainly and more deplorably, the womanly face and expression?

How far these heats of partisanship will go in dissolving ultimately the bonds of delicacy and the proprieties of good manners, it may not be easy to say, but it is at least impossible that the moralities should keep their present footing. It is part of the reform, that women are to be candidates themselves perhaps equally with men, and so many, with their special friends and allies, will of course be thrown upon waves of excitement and put to a strain of principle intensely severe. And if men, as we hear, will sell every thing at the polls for success, it is not to be doubted that women will show like mortal infirmities. Coming out of their now vestal retirement to make friends and political capital, we shall hear what kind of bargains this or that woman is arranging, and how she manages what is called the "dirty work" of her canvass. They must come of course to this, else how can they get on? If they take the stump, woman against woman, or woman against man, it will only be a much better figure to be in, than the button-holing and private colloding with gentlemen, going on so often in back rooms and by-places. Or if we say nothing of the perils of candidacy, and only speak of the vote, women as a general thing do not make good partisans. They over feel, over-contrive, over-do, and in this manner weaken morally themselves and their cause. It masters them so totally that both it and they appear badly. They let in also little malignancies that are poisonous, and get their motive so twisted in with their dislikes and animosities, that they are a great way further off from the integrities of their cause than they know themselves. They become viragos in this manner when they think they are only doing all in righteous vehemence.

We also know that women often show a strange facility of debasement and moral abandonment, when they have once given way consentingly to wrong. Men go down by a descent—*facilis descensus*—women, by a precipitation. Perhaps the reason is, in part, that more is expected of women and that again because there is more expectancy of truth and sacrifice in the semi-christly, subject state of women than is likely to be looked for in the forward, self-asserting headship of men. Be it as it may, the simple fact that more is expected of women, whether more should be or not, shows that when they do wrong, they have more to face, on which account they fall as much faster and lower. It must therefore be expected, when this reform against nature is carried, that we shall have a great deal more of a great deal worse corruption in our public affairs, than we have now. And the opposite confidence many boast is far more nearly preposterous than it need be. If we could take our present women at their present point of beauty or of unsophisticated good, and bring them directly into political life with us, having corps of angels in company, to salt them and keep them in their present state of disinterested good, they would give us prime benefit doubtless, by their aid. But the difficulty is, that angels have other work to do, and that we have no salt strong enough for that kind of keeping—the women will change; not immediately, but after a time, such as will permit the corrupting causes to do their work, becoming finally exactly what they now are not. Make no doubt of it, women are venal as truly as men; a great deal more easily preyed upon by art and cheated by stratagem. As they sooner believe they are sooner made a prey of. And they will only suffer the more from the art, the stratagem, the prey, that they go to the practice of it themselves and get the fair, sweet motives of their womanhood mixed up with so many obliquities. As certainly as women are human, and none of us have any doubt of that, they will take in the political corruptions with a prone-minded human facility. Nor is it any fit answer to say, that they have as good right as men to be in such corruptions, provided they are not in worse. They will be in worse; a woman can not be as bad as a man in any thing, without being worse; for a selfish, plotting, intriguing, political, make-shift woman has a great deal more of the fine fair stuff to mar and muddle in becoming what she is, than a man will have. And then again, when the two are nearly at the same level of baseness and trickery, the man will have a firmer will and keep his self-retention evenly enough to almost make it seem a kind of virtue; whereas often the partridge-like fuss and commotion, by which a woman clucks down her brood of stratagems, makes her art more visible and artful, and she is just so much the more corrupted by it. True, it is pretense or smooth disguise in both cases. Hence also it is that we so often hear of slimy men; God grant that we may not be obliged to hear as much more still of slimy women.

But we shall better understand what we are discussing, if we look a little farther in upon the political machinery, and see how it works in preparing and executing the operation of the suffrage. The great, the almost insuperable difficulty encountered now in our scheme of suffrage, is that the primary assemblies, those which select and set up the candidates, are so generally filled up, in the large cities and towns, by a rush of all the worst, most abandoned, most violent characters. Good men, men of respect and order can do nothing there, they are wholly out of place. The mob—for it is the mob only that has the tempest in hand—hears no reason, bawls, stamps, raves, roars, and pitches into fisticuffs, getting first the organization by getting all decencies under, and then the business goes on. And if you ask who will be nominated, why exactly they undoubtedly who bought, or some way made friends of the mob before they came together.

But there is to come in now, as we propose, another element, viz., women; and there will be women who expect to be candidates. And how? Of course they must buy, or somehow make court to their mob also. They can have one too, if they will, as noisy, and base, and violent, though made up of women, as any worst and wildest crew of men. Matters will come along then somewhat in this way—certain managing men will manage certain managing women, and a few of these managing women can empty whole streets of women into any primary assembly, and have them take their part as warmly as can be desired.

Possibly it will come out as the result in a way of concession to the respectables, that a candidate or two, male or female, is put up who has a tolerable show of character; and besides that a much larger number have the kind of character, better called no character, which made them favorites and leaders of their mob. At the head of the whole operation, as the ticket now goes to the polls, there is probably some master demagogue, having two or three subordinates that manipulate the process with him, and they make their headquarters, privately of course, at some palace of vice, where some gilded woman undertakes with them to farm the managing women subordinate, and they to bring out and lead their general crew.

The woman, or women of character on the ticket have the gilded woman aforesaid not unlikely with them on the same, and a good many others, all no better than they should be, and they run all together for Congress, or the General Assembly, or the Common Council. The better candidates must not stick at their company of course, or any way bolt the ticket. And then, when the voting women come to the ballot, they must think it sufficient that there is some worthy character on the ticket; and if they suffer it to be suspected that they will not vote the unworthy, they must expect to be dogged by the argument of damage and destruction to the party, and must learn, if possible, to swallow their scruples, and vote the reigning harlot and the reigning philanthropist or true woman together.

Now, it will seem quite improbable, I suppose, to the inexperienced, that any so revolting contingencies are likely to arise. Better far, to ask, How it is possible for them not to arise? The scenes and occasions described answer exactly to what occurs every year, in the large towns and great cities, where the male suffrage is called for, and it is understood by everybody that the hell of a nominating assembly is the worst hell above ground, anywhere to be seen. And do you ask, What shall make it more certainly better, than that a full half of the assembly is to be made up of women? Are there no bad women, then? And where will they go to be more at home and behave worse, than amid the uproar and tumult of so many wild and brutal men?

It sounds very pleasantly, doubtless, when some talented, high woman, is spoken of as put up, on her quiet merit, for the vote of the people. But that is pure hallucination. No such thing is possible. She must get the nomination, strong enough to carry her in, within the party lines; and if any one imagines that she can go into the primary assemblies, and be heard there among the gods of the abyss, they have only to put her on trying it, to find out how utterly absurd any such thing may be. In such a city as Hartford, for example, it will be found, within a ten-years' time after this reform is passed, that the nominations will be half determined by just this woman element, and that no true woman has any least chance of a nomination, save as somebody engineers for it, and is pitched into the lions' den to obtain it. And then most likely the fair candidate will find herself on a ticket with names that put her in a class with dishonor itself. Still, if she is going to be a politician, she must not be delicate about her associations!

But we must go to the scene of the ballot itself, and see what is likely to be seen there. We sometimes hear it proposed that the women shall have boxes provided for their particular vote, in some quiet place by themselves, and it seems to be imagined that they will go there as to a pic-nic, or a sewing-circle. One of our literary gentlemen, too, has this matter of women's suffrage, I perceive, in so light a key, that he compares the ballot-box to a post-office box, and thinks it a question of as little concern what one will do for a woman as the other. Exactly contrary to this, I am ready to predict that the woman's box, within a very few years, will become worse and more unmanageable than the man's. The crew that are gathered around it will be more disorderly, and less respectful of decency; and partly so for the reason, that they have so much larger opportunities of frauds. I make nothing here of what has been reported as regards the fraud of the voting women at the polls in New Jersey, the fine opportunity for which was so very soon discovered. Any one can see for himself, that the dress of women is of a kind to permit of infinite disguises, and such, too, as forbid even a possibility of detection. The whole crew of unprincipled women can be brought on thus, six or eight times over, at any election, having only changes of dress provided for the personation of as many characters. And the man-poll, bad as it is, will be honesty itself, in comparison. Other modes of demoralization will also be discovered, especially in the country and the more sparsely settled parts, where men and women will be piled in huge wagons to be carried to the polls, and will sometimes, on their return, encounter a storm that drives them into wayside taverns and other like places, for the night; where, of course, they must have a good time somehow, probably in some kind of general carouse that will comfort their defeat, or celebrate their victory. Finally, the next day the women voters are put down at home—with some things to regret, which are only worse if not regretted. Indeed, this herding of the two sexes together in political action involves no small danger of a frequent drinking together, in the lower tiers of society, than which almost nothing could have a more disastrous effect.

We must also follow this matter still farther in another direction. This conjunction of the sexes in political life makes it almost a matter of course that an immense lobby of fair women should be gathered about the halls of Congress and the State legislatures, there to manipulate causes, and measures, and men, as they will know how, shielded by their own numbers and the public gloss of a conjoined action of the two sexes. All these great bodies of legislation will become, in this manner, as many courts of the Bourbons, and the general game will be to settle what women are to have the patronages, keep the treasury keys, and do the public fleecing of the people. And if any one imagines that the representative women inside of these great bodies, Congress for example, will be acting correctively, as a counter-check to such corruptions outside, it is certainly a comfort most welcome to hope as much, if we may. I wish we could be more sure of it. First of all, the women that are inside have a considerable chance of being no better than the women outside; and then, if they are, it does not clearly appear in what matter they are likely to exert much power. For a time they will be treated with <u>consideration</u>, because they are women, and when that kind of <u>delicacy is worn off</u>, and they are left to take their equal chance with men, as their great reform itself proposes, they will find that getting the floor and holding it in that bear-garden, is about as nearly impossible as it can be. At the end of twenty years no living woman can do it. She must not over-strain her treble, if she does, there will be laughter. If she shakes herself in great resolve, puts on force, grows immensely emphatic, denounces, satirises, as a man might do, with not a whit more talent and even conquering applause and a place by it, if perchance she takes on but a very faint show of the vixenish manner, that will be the end of her. The truth is, <u>that women are not made to govern men</u>; as will here, if not sooner, be discovered. And when the woman power has given out thus in the Congress, and the discouraged representatives are finally discontinued, the moral collapse of the reform will be sadly evident. And the specially sad thing of all will be, that a catastrophe so conspicuous and so boldly challenged, will let down, far too low, the just respect of woman. That respect can be, and is in fact now being, raised, if we let the suffrage question pass; when, if we go on to put her on that test, we simply break the neck of all her possibility across it. Her true good and glory do not lie in being a man with men, but in being more completely and sufficiently woman. Would that we could simply see, for one single century, what powers of industry, and thought, and art, and beauty, and immortal insight, can be unfolded in a full round culture of woman; that I am quite sure would effectually raise her condition, and put her in a scale of honor, where all mere place and office would seem to be in a lower plane.

I ought perhaps in fairness, to suggest, that a reconstruction of our government is conceivable, that would obviate some of the mischiefs here referred to. If there were a second or third house, called the House of Women, interposed between our Senate and Representative chambers, in such a way that any measure could originate in either, and every measure must pass the vote of the three, this would give full opportunity to the women to look after their own affairs, and after all fit legislations by which they may best advance their condition. But this would give them a legislative power, when it really does not belong, as we have seen, to their womanly nature to govern, and would also give them a practical veto over all the governing rights of men. Whether this would satisfy is doubtful also; and if it would, the immense and really frightful difficulty of the primary assemblies still remains, and I see not how it can be obviated.

But there is a very deep, not improbable connection between this matter of women's suffrage and the family state, where it is likely to have a dangerously demoralizing power. I have purposely abstained in this discussion from any particular notice of the physiological subtractions that so largely disqualify women for an active and forward part in political affairs. I have not insisted on the inequalities of their temperaments, or the incapacities to which they are subject, or the mischiefs that may come upon children through an ante-natal and post-natal nurture of two whole years and more, disturbed in all that time by states of political excitement. Passing all these, and a hundred matters of the kind, I will simply refer to some of the reasons we have for apprehending a relaxation of the just bonds of marriage, and a greatly increased tendency, first to avoid marriage, and secondly to obtain divorce. It is even remarkable that the very point of departure in the women's suffrage argument reduces marriage to a mere partnership contract. Thus it is denied a hundred times a day in these discussions, that there is "any more reason why the woman should take her husband's name in marriage than why he should take hers." All which goes on the principle that the two are, in every sense, equal; that the woman is just as much head of the man as the man of the woman; that he is given as truly to be her helpmate as she to be his, and that all the physiological distinctions we see with our eyes, which exactly declare the scripture doctrine over again, are insignificant and of no account. The two therefore come together not to be one, a total nature, which is marriage, but to be two in equal contract, which is partnership. Of course the partnership contract may be terminated, as all other contracts may, by the parties themselves. It is no *quasi* sacrament, no mystic bond of God that puts the parties in their places and parts, one to be responsible for the forwarding and outside provisioning of their lot, the other to be retired and subject inside for the comforting, and right keeping, and due ornament and order of life. All this goes by under the remorseless ditto of an equality never beheld in the world, and which, dropping revelation out of sight, is the poorest conceivable fiction. Is there any thing more visible than that here are two kinds, say what we will of the equalities? Is there not a man and woman, and are not the two a complete one? And is not the man as visibly head of that oneness as any head set upon two shoulders was ever head of the body? Partnerships have no head in this way, because

7*

the ditto principle exactly levels the parties. Marriage has and is to have, must have, a head, and a connecting bond that runs down through, else it is a thing gone by.

And here is the melancholy fact, as regards this boasted reform, that it loosens every joint of the family state, and is really meant to do it, as we plainly see by many of the appeals set forth. Thus a leading woman apostle of this reform gives out for her declared sentiment, that "true marriage, like true religion, dwells in the sanctuary of the soul, beyond the cognizance or sanction of state or church;" ridicules the notion that a man's wife " is his property if once married, no matter whether her affections are his or another's;" laughs at his indignations, "if any one else has dared to call out what he never could;" and finally, as if to stir up discontent with marriage, in a way of enlisting the discontented in her cause, exclaims— "Oh, what a sham is the marriage we see about us, though sanctioned in our courts, and baptized at our altars, where cunning priests take toll for binding virtue with vice, angels of grace and goodness with devils in malice and malignity; beauty with deformity, joyous youth with gilded old age —palsied, blasted, with nothing to give its victim in white veil and orange blossoms but a state of luxury and sensualism." Whether these citations are meant to be as shocking as they certainly are, I do not know, and it is of no great importance to inquire. Enough to see what kind of *animus* struggles in the utterance, and that marriage is gone down forever in the argument and reform, that are working their way by appeals so revolting. Nobody can talk in this way of marriage, who would not head a general coming out of it, and is not ready to offer that kind of leadership.

Any one can see that a reform thus carried, carries with it discontent with marriage, and to just the same extent insures a legislation to facilitate divorce. Nobody is to blame, in this kind of casuistry, for the bad marriages, but the priests and the laws, and the woman party has a right of course to be quit, as soon as new passions rise to ask it, or the old ones die to make it a riddance. Being perfectly equal, and put upon her equality with her husband for the right to vote, she must prove her equality somehow, when she comes to the voting and how shall she do it, but by asserting her independence in a vote upon the other side? Such contrary vote need not do any fatal harm, it is true, and yet there is a loosening touch in it, so that if some feeling of hurt has been stirred by hot passages of debate before, or may be afterward, there is a considerable beginning of divorce in it. No wise scheme of polity will consentingly multiply such occasions of damage, in a relation at once so sacred and so delicate. Besides, where the two parties in marriage are known to be opposite in their party affinities, there will be private collodings sought, that will greatly expose the frailty of the woman, and as greatly tempt the jealousy of the man. Sometimes when the husband is up as a candidate, an opposing party, who are willing to see mischief, will set up his wife against him, and whether she consents or not, will run her into the major vote, on purpose to put him in derision. Sometimes a wife in bad blood will get herself nominated against her husband, for the purpose of bringing him under contempt and preparing the divorce she wants.

The general scheme of women's suffrage works against marriage, as we thus perceive, to make it less sacred and less permanent and just as much less beneficial. Frequent divorces check the rate of populations, as the Romans found to their cost. Frequent divorces are the bane of all family peace and order before they come, and the extinction of all true family life and nurture after they come. Hapless beings, too, are the children, that being heirs just now to a parentage and a home, are only heirs henceforth to a family quarrel. Now the dear feeling they had of their parentage is succeeded by the only question left, viz.: Who was to blame? which if they can settle it brings no comfort, and which, if they can not, brings scarcely less. Sad and decadent is the history of any people who have forgotten how to sanctify marriage, and whose children go to the records of divorce instead of the records of marriage, to find their fathers and mothers.

I spoke in my preliminary chapter of the very galling and terrible hardships falling on woman, by reason of the scanty prices paid for her labor. No friend who desires to improve her condition, or take off the real oppressions under which she is crushed, will be in a mood, as it seems to me, to reject almost any kind of reform that promises the needed relief. Perhaps we are able now to see a little more distinctly what kind of help will do it, and what will not. The women's suffrage reform will not, of course, make employers less greedy, or workers more capable, or work more abundant. Or, if the transference of a few women to public offices and functions would bring a very little relief, that same relief can be quite as easily secured, under the present mode of government, without any change. It is being largely secured now, and is regarded by the whole people only with favor. A very great work may be done to raise the prices of female industry by advancing, in every way possible, the education of women, and so their capacity of more, and better, and more various kinds of work. Also, by efforts, public and private, to conserve the morality of husbands and fathers, and save their hapless families from being precipitated, in such multitude, upon the labor market, to obtain their pittance of bread; also, by endeavors to encourage and promote early marriages among industrious and virtuous young people in humble life—but so far, nothing is wanted plainly of the great reform we are now proposing, and it does not appear that any thing good will come of it. If it is expected that women going into the legislatures will enact a new tariff of prices for women's labor, that is one of the things which no monarch or assembly of men was ever able to do, and it is not likely that women will do it. If it could be made to appear that women, going into conditions of public office and power, would obtain consideration, and a just weight of character for the sex, that would undoubtedly do something for the current prices of woman's labor; for the higher place of public estimation they hold, the more highly rated, or appreciated will their service be. And, probably, a good deal more can be done, in this way, than has been hitherto, by putting women in offices that involve no governing right—post-offices and clerkships, for example—and this can be done as well without the right of vote, and the right of rule, as with. But why not, on the same principle, give them a right to vote, and a right to rule also. Will not that also raise our impressions of their capacity and value? I think not. On the contrary, it is my fixed belief that, as woman is not set for the government of men by nature, the whole reform, taken in the long run of time, will do the very utmost possible to break down the honor of women, and put them at a lower standing than now. The very thing preparing is a grand mortal failure, under which the sex will be a great deal more depressed and discouraged, than it would under any worst persecution. Governing women, rely upon it, are never going to be in fashion. There is a sentence against it, written so deep down in nature, that not all women and all men together can take it finally away.

Any hope, therefore, of raising woman's lot and woman's prices, by putting this dower of authority upon her, will assuredly result in a terrible reaction, that will pitch her down a gulf which, as far as we can see, admits no lift of recovery. The tracks going hither turn all one way, and I see not now how they can ever be reversed. Broken down by such a failure, prices and respect and many other things go down, and no countervailing possibility of reform is left.

I can not close this computation of the effects of women's suffrage without noting also the immense loss of sentiment and character that will result from it. It will be a greater loss to us of the male sex than we can now realize, or even distinctly imagine. Our advocates of women's suffrage, Mr. Beecher among them, have much to say, and certainly not too much of the "moral refinement," and culture of men by "the co-ordinate influence of woman." But it is not observed, as it should be, that the power we thus get on our masculine character is not so much from what women do to us, as from what we do to them. They do much upon us, it is true, by their gentle and fine qualities, and the close association by which they get a kind of inhabitation in us for their own more delicate spirit; and yet the main thing with us, the grand civilizing efficacy consists, in a principal degree, in what we are doing to them, the courtesies we practice and the homages we spontaneously pay. We are taken clean by our masculine selfishness here, to pay a tribute as it were, in the bending of our force unto what is not in force, and we feel ourselves blessed and exalted in the geniality and conscious pleasure of our homages. We observe a common looking man, for example, standing in a railroad car, that a common looking woman may sit, and we say inwardly, at least, if not audibly, "there is yet, after all, some hope of the world." Now it is not true, perhaps, that that said woman is doing any thing specially on that said man, unless by a certain grace of thanks which beams in her eye—probably he knows nothing about her, and has never felt, and never will, any quality that she has; and yet he is doing for himself upon her what will repay his inconveniences a hundred times over. And these beautiful deferences and homages paid to women are the very best civilizers we have, and we can better afford to spare almost any thing else. They are no mere by-play, or fancy-play as, many foolishly think, but they are, in fact, strong, shaping powers, that are forming the manners, and fining the grain, and raising in fact the very consciousness of our sex. Does any one believe that women standing for equality, asking no more for any thing but to measure powers with us, protesting that they want no patronage, and consenting to let us have our courtesies to ourselves, if only they may set their equal manhood alongside of us—does any one miss perceiving the immense loss we must suffer, and how it carries off with it all the highest flavors of our life. Selfishness, barbarism, aridity—what but these are left, when every beautiful courtesy we loved to pay to women is dead?

And there is a loss upon the other side that is scarcely less deplorable. When a woman has set herself up for a practical dittoship with men, refusing to accept the name of her husband, or have any but a partnership relation with him, she ceases so far to be woman at all. She has no longer the trusting nature, she despises it, she neither idolizes nor idealizes her husband. She has no homages looking up, any more than he, in his ranges of force, has courtesies to pay her looking down. He is gruff, and she is pungent, and the main sensibility of life is the friction of it. She has gotten now a right to vote, and a right, if she can, to get office; and has it for the chief congratulation of her new state that she is now one of the world's combatant forces. Hereafter she fights on her own hook, and will be as much a man as she likes; or, what is more probable, as much a man as she can be. The beauty of her womanly state and feeling, all the dear specialties of wifehood are gone by, and she takes her life no more in sentiments, but in ostrich-like rampages over the desert she is left to occupy.

It can not be so, I perceive, to many, but to me these sexhood qualities of variation, this dovetailing of sentiment by unlikeness of kind, so by deferences, homages, admirations, worships, doings in excess of right, and estimations in excess of merit, is the very fairest side of all fair beauty in the world. There is a delicate hand and a rough, strong hand; there is a voice above answered by a voice in octave below; there is an indoor life and quality, and an out-door that will have concern with the world; what each is, the other wants, and they both get away from the mere stale fact of what they are, by idolizing each other, playing at or into all diversities, and all diversities into more and better. Call it the state of inequality, if we please; it is yet such inequality that no one knows in which the superiority may be. It is that state composed by complementary inequalities which we can least afford to lose; and if there is any thing over which the word *accursed* can be fitly written, it is over the remorseless, mock-equalizing, that is going to make so many peas, or flaxseeds of human people grow into the same exact figure, and be, in every two, the double, each, of the other. I see nothing but starvation in that kind of equality; and we all shall know it thus, with regrets unspeakable, after this proposed reform has been long enough carried to prove what is in it. Looking back, as we shall, from such a condition attained, on our present state of interplay—boldness and modesty, governing and trust, the fresh delectations and varieties weaving our web of life—it will even seem to be a kind of paradise, though it be a paradise under evil. If any thing indeed remains to be lost by a second fall, it will be our exclusion from this evil-tainted paradise, by the very dismal kind of society against nature, and equality in one color, which it is here proposed to create.

VIII.

PROSPECTS AND POSSIBILITIES OF WOMEN.

To have been confronted, in the argument of this question, by some treatise or discussion that deliberately stated and expounded the speculative doctrine of the side opposite, would have been a considerable help. But unfortunately the debate, if such it can be called, has hitherto been carried on by extempore speeches, popular magazine articles, and brief random effusions of the press, that were concerned, first of all, to fulfill the conditions of piquancy, and not to unfold the solid reason of the question. Hence it has been difficult, to be sure that the mode of exposition here attempted was going to meet any sufficiently deliberative opinion held, in respect to the rational grounds of the reform proposed. For this reason I have been hoping, partly waiting, for the forthcoming book promised by Mr. Mill. But it does not yet arrive.

It is understood that he takes the side of the proposed reform, as he naturally enough would under his particular bent of philosophy; for it is not his manner to have any principal respect to categories, absolute properties, or laws of kind that are immovable, but to see all things, even the distinctions of morality, developed and shaped by the contingent, variable operations of experience. What, in this view, is a woman, but a man kept down or badly hindered, or somehow insufficiently developed? And then what else are we to think of, but the higher development she will attain to, when her equal rights in the state are acknowledged, and her equal opportunity in public life is secured? The title of his book, therefore, as I think I have somewhere seen, is "*The Subject Condition of Women.*" Under which it will naturally be held, as by Mrs. Mill in her somewhat noted article in the *Westminster Review*, that the subject state of women, down to this time, is due in no sense to a subject nature, but wholly to matters conditional. Indeed the precise issue between us here, which I am quite willing to accept, is whether woman is subject as having a subject nature, or subject as being held down by politically oppressive conditions? If the former, she is not going of course to be helped over and by her nature, and raised up thus into forwardness and a way of command—she will be subject still, even if she is set in the Presidency, and will govern only as a subject nature can. If the latter, she will as certainly not be raised into a manly, governing way, because she has no capacity of being thus raised by any conditions whatever.

No conceivable improvement in her social and political conditions will bring her up into the force-element and make her a self-centered, governing, driving-engine character—which appears to be the kind of merit aspired to. Her conditions will not create a man's nerve in her, but she will only have a woman's still as now, and the very development into which she is pushed will be a woman's development, as far as it is any thing. Rightly developed she will be a mere complete woman, but not a whit less subject, or a whit more nearly even with man, in that which belongs to his particular kind of eminence.

It is remarkable, when so much is made or to be made, of condition, that it does not occur to reformers who take this mode of argument, to ask why it is, from the creation downward, that women have fallen into a condition of so great disadvantage? Perhaps they will say, as they often do when their point is to raise an accusation, and not to account for the fact referred to, that man was endued originally with greater strength of person, or superior physical force, and that he has trampled woman, in this manner, because he could, and shut her down under conditions of great incapacity and discouragement. And this undoubtedly is true, or at least far more widely and sadly true than it should be, though not so entirely or totally true as to exclude the fact that such superior strength is loving, none the less, among every people of the world, to bow itself to such inferior, in beautiful acts of championship and protection, securing thus to women a condition of comfort and respect they could never secure for themselves. But if we let the case be as bad as this kind of argument supposes, and take it as the fact of history that women have been everywhere oppressed by the superior force of men, this at least will be clear, as conceded by the argument itself, that men originally had this gift or endowment of a larger stature and a far superior muscular force. It may not be any very high distinction, but such as it is they have it, and in having it are men. Besides, in this more massive and crude sort of endowment, we are to see that, as they are in force, so their force is the housing and expression of their natural authority. It signifies government, or governing capacity and order, and just as impressively the relatively subject nature of women. And so we come out in the discovery that women, after all, are in a subject nature, and not merely in a subject condition—they are relatively frail and delicate, in a finer type of grace and color, a less coarse, stormy voice, and with a different innerving quality which is distinctively feminine. And this we may think it more respectful to call the subject condition of women and not the subject nature, though if we mean to thoroughly understand ourselves, how far off is it from being, in any view possible, a subject nature?

However, there can be very few thoughtful persons, I imagine, who are not sometimes caught with impressions of quality, and glimpses of possibility in this subject nature, that are exceedingly high—shall I say, transcendently high? But a few evenings since, reclining in a room two doors removed from the parlor where two young friends were having their good time, in the pleasant conversation of a call, I was caught by a strange feeling of surprise, in the simple overhearing of their sounds, when I could not distinguish a word of their utterance. The male voice went off with a thud, as if there were some center point of self assertion whence it issued, and some base line of purpose along which the missile was to go. It varied a little, but only a little in pitch, and went ranging along the lower lines of the stave, not as if there were quaverings of sensibility in it, but as if it were a solid, going straight by its own momentum. There was energy in it, and it raised the sense of will and of power, but the reverberative guttural, or pectoral, was not of a specially winsome quality, for the drive there was in it was just a little undivine. At any rate nobody is going back of it, to put any shred of better meaning, or note of better music into it. It begins from itself, and is going to have its way. Meantime the other voice, how supremely better and how beautifully turned! It is modesty and gentle deference converted into sound. It rises and waves and carols and goes fluting and caracoling round the other, over and under, even as a vine might spin its graces and benignities about a rock. It is as if some better nature had arrived from some better, more unselfish world, and were trying, in what manner it can, to gain the grim monotone force, and twist some charm of heaven's music into its feeling. Perhaps, if the words had been audible, a very different impression would have been taken, but the mere sounds themselves were saying, as it seemed,— "this for you, not for myself."

This now is the subject nature, and the other is the forward governing nature; and the promise of our new reform is that, if the woman can but find a better and more equal condition in the world of political scramble, and so be duly developed, she will make as high a creature, well nigh, as the other! I see nothing to attract, I confess, in that kind of promise. On the contrary it seems quite impossible to keep off the conviction of some latent property in the woman, that will some time place her far above the coarse, crass, self-will precedence in which the masculine vigor is thought to be so impressively displayed. On this ground, I object most emphatically to any stirring up of discontent in women with their lot. It is simple cruelty, for their lot is at bottom, their own nature itself—that and nothing else. And it is a nature glorious in its beauty, which they can not afford to infringe by any disrespect, and should most consentingly accept and hopefully cultivate. A discontented woman quarreling with her womanhood, which neither she nor all angels can change, nor any good angel could even wish to change—what thing more wretched, and wicked, and weak, and absurd can well be conceived. True it is a subject nature, but it is the most honorable, finest, highest nature, in many of its qualities and capabilities it has ever been given us to know.

It seems to me that we are quite blind as yet to the true sphere of woman and the possible degree of her advancement, and that, partly for this reason, we are now campaigning to get her out of her subject condition as we call it, and make a man of her. We tell her that she belongs to the "Suppressed Sex," and we really think so—just because we have not learned as yet to think any thing better and higher ourselves. We do not perceive the vast woman-field she is filling and to sometime fill, with a luster wholly her own; which, too, she must just so far abandon, as she begins to emulate the masculine spheres and aspire to the masculine offices. Let us see, if we can, whether women can stay by their womanhood and have any true great hope in it.

It may be true that we hear enough said of the motherhood office and the immense practical import of it. A very dull wit can expatiate on this theme, and we are dosed *ad nauseum*, as we sometimes think, with this prosing kind of sentiment.

But there is a magnificent maternal honor incorporate here, which I do not remember ever to have seen mentioned, and which ought to give all women an immensely good opinion of the womanly nature, subject though it be. I look upon it, I confess, with even a kind of awe. It is not a self-asserting but a naturally worshipful and client nature, that delights to sink itself out of sight and so far to be in another; and in just this fact it is elected to be the nurse of the world's childhood. As the world is selfish, and the child, doing every best thing for it, is likely to be hopelessly devoured by that kind of frenzy, unless the mitigations derivable from some more benignant element may save it, in a degree, for God's better occupancy—for this reason, all motherhood is gathered about all childhood in a subject nature, to be a kind of first gospel in the flesh, and savor it, as it were, beforehand. The child is born into the lap of a covert, gladly worshipful motherhood; drinks in patience, reverence, subordination, to the one idea of the family headship, and is so to be partially configured to the grand moral headship of the Supreme Father. And hence it is that motherhoods obtain such ineradicable, inexpugnable possession of the life of sons and daughters. Fathers have a certain power and are held in dear respect. But it is the subject nature of motherhood, the patient, self-forgetting element it makes, that fastens a feeling so deep in the child. If these mothers were all out as campaigners, intriguers, and would-be statesmen, it would not cost their sons a great deal of trouble to forget them. After this new dispensation arrives, when party cabal and the intrigues of selfish ambition become the proper element of women, the wayward sons will no more be tethered, as now, to good, by the remembrances of their almost divine motherhood.

We very commonly imagine, when we speak of dress as one of the rather weak foibles of women, that there is or can be no dignity or high value in it. There certainly is an abundant show of nonsense, and sometimes of a most real and contemptible selfishness, in what is called fashion. And if our beautiful sisterhood want to conquer their emancipation from a great and terrible thralldom, here is their opportunity. To get emancipated from men, or the political sovereignty of men in the State, is a very small matter and a victory quite insignificant, compared with this. And if they greatly admire the masculine nerve displayed in public affairs, let them understand that very many men have not the nerve to defy or cast off a fashion; so that if they are resolute and brave enough to conquer, in this kind of battle, they can do what many great commanders never were able. And exactly this huge overthrow must some time hence be carried; for it is the weakest, most despotic, and cruel kind of empire ever endured by mortals. The day is coming—

let our women see that it is duly hastened—when taste will be so far advanced as to be the supreme arbiter of dress in every person. Dress will then be seen to be just what it is: viz., a fine art of the highest order, and related even to the supreme beauty of all character. Who of us have not seen examples of just this wonderful kind of beauty? It shows the sense of fitness, or properness, to be supreme, and reveals the internal mode of a beautiful soul by just that which is the natural outgo of expression. Such is dress. Is there any thing finer, lovelier, more fascinating, and, in fact, more indicative of the great possible advance to be made, when the souls and characters of women get in grace and culture enough for such a kind of excellence. Here is nothing gotten up by the cheap methods of shop-women studying their cards. Here is no dash of diamonds a half million strong, the tricking of a dowdy, or the shower of glitter in which a really fair woman dissolves her beauty and makes a nothing of it; but there is modesty, there is figure that appears to have come of itself, the draperies and colors are all fit—right in quantity, right in limitation—because there was character and culture enough to bring just this to pass without knowing it.

Giving such an estimate of dress, and its importance in the scale of human advancement, I may seem to hold an egregious opinion of its value. But it must be remembered, first, that what we now call dress, and deprecate as extravagance, is not dress at all—only a very few persons know what dress really means, or how it comes, and we have but the faintest ideas therefore of that high figure, in which the true society of the world is some time to appear. And again, secondly, we must not forget that there is a most intimate and living connection between dress on one hand, and manners and society on the other. The forms of appearing and action include the article of dress, with its true refinements and proprieties, in common with all that belongs to personal behavior and to the general way and manner of society. And here it is that woman has her kingdom. Subject in the state, she is qualified, in just that fact, to be the queen of society. And is society nothing, do we think? Are there no honors and powers and quantities of well-being here at stake? Why, there is more to be determined, legislated, done, enjoyed, and lost, in this great matter of society, than there is in all the enactments, executive offices, and judicial decisions of the state, many times over. Is it then to be imagined that the world-famous women, the Miss Marshalls, the Mrs. Madisons, the Madame Recamiers, the Madame Swetchines, and a thousand other queens that, being good or less good, gather princes and multitudes about the queenly centers they make and the beautiful graces in which they shine, are, in fact, doing nothing for their country or mankind? Just contrary to this, it is they, even more than the male magistracies, that are fashioning the world. Aspasia is more than Pericles a hundred times over; because he governs only the state, and she governs both the governors of the state and the people beside. Happy is that people that can make society. Lacedemon could as little make it as a den of bears. Athens could have it because it had a woman. Great thing it is for any people that they can have society; thought ennobled, art become a joy, good and pure manners, lofty and true sentiment, delicacy, beauty, great aspirations, a state above the state, that which no man ever made or swayed, but which only women, one or many, could. It requires just what we have been calling a subject nature to prepare society. There are no kings here but only queens. All partisans and men of power are incapable of this kind of dominion. It supposes what is more catholic, another law moving in another line, where truth, and right, and beauty, and right inspirations, and manners that have come to the flower, create a new, great element of general fellowship, and true public love.

We are trying just now every possible or impossible way of reducing our public vices, and especially our all-demoralizing drink. The state fairly staggers politically under the problem, finding no way. No way, I fear, is ever coming by the legislative, "be-it-enacted" method. But what the state can not do, society can; and society will do it, whenever the great women arise to make society in that high key. And they will do it by no denunciatory action; but by simply making a right, clean atmosphere, which no beast can willingly defile; consecrating character by its dignities, life by its moralities, and putting all the elegancies in cast, by good and true inspirations. Only the subject condition can address itself to these ignominies of life. Legal prohibitions, fines, imprisonments, have only such remedial efficacy as God's own law has had in the mending of transgression.

It has never yet been sufficiently seen what stores of poetry are hid in the light-moving, tenderly-fibered, subject nature of women. The bane of all great poetry is self-recollection, and the letting in of will to do what only true inspirations can. And exactly here is the point where so many breaks and falls occur. The man ventures, in some unlucky moment, to make his appearance himself—putting in his force to conquer, when force has no such power. His performance gets a spacing, in this manner, of insipidities and little defections, that more or less fatally take him down. His will, in fact, even though he may not see it, is, poetically speaking, the weakest, lowest faculty he has. But as men expect to govern by their will, and do many things in the habit of putting their will into them, it will be all the more difficult not to fall sometimes into the way of manufacturing verses, when they think they are writing poetry. Is it not a matter of fair expectation that, when the women of an age not far off, find where the inspirations are, and set their nimble, fine-strung harps in play, they will give us modes of thought and sentiment and wonders of perception, more ethereal and closer to the living fiber of souls than we have hitherto known? The very fact that women are in a smaller and more delicate key, will permit their wings to carry them higher, and will let us hear them empty their music into the sky, clear above where our male larks and eagles have been able in the past times to go. And let not this appear extravagant, for our women certainly have not yet found their wings. Are we not able to see, by a mere glance of the eye, that they have a nature fibered and feathered for the highest inspirations, whenever they can think and believe, in a key to reach their own possibilities?

These auguries will be largely confirmed, if we advert to the closely kindred art of music. Why is it, we may ask, that men's voices, larger in quantity and sometimes wonderfully fine in quality, are yet never able to produce the same or any proximate effects compared with the voices of women? Not all the kings and queens of the old world, with all the high magistrates of the new, had more than a hundredth part of the impression, accent, sway in men's feeling, that a single singing woman lately had, in the memory of us all. No such power was ever held by any singing man, or ever will be. And the reason is not, as we assume so often, that the soprano voice is of course more effective. No; the true reason is that the man lets himself into his singing, forces his voice, puts his will into the modulations, and lets us see that he is, all the while, conscious of what he is doing. Having thunders of government and self-centered energy in him, he must needs play on his voice, and finger, as it were, the stops of it himself. Many times it will be even visible that, having the finest possible organ, he never once caught the idea of an inspiration, or a free gale wafting him on, in his life. He sings velocipede-wise, turning the crank himself. If there is a liquid element in his nature, he has never let his heart down where it is, but he sings a song of surfaces by his will, and the self-modulation of his art—very dry, made up of single notes and pieces jolted together without flow. But the woman has a better nature for this matter. She is less supremely, less indivertibly selfish. Her subject will is not always on hand, to put her fussing consciously at her modulations. She takes the inspirations easily and without knowing it, and has the tingle of the sentiment in her whole person. Grace, beauty, life, love, beam and glow and blend and rise, and her audiences are carried away, they scarce know whither. Is there any greater eminence of power in any political magistracy, or official promotion of the world? And if we take these two together, poetry and music, and consider the grand possibilities of advancement offered thereby to the genius of women—possibilities never yet unfolded as they sometimes will be—we shall not be in haste to set them on riots of appeal to conquer places that will give significance to their life. Had Alboni been able to get herself installed in the Intendancy of the Revenue of Ancona, or Jenny Lind to get the place of Port Warden at Gottenburg, I do not see that their political successes would have done much for them.

There is yet another vast field of endeavor for women which ought to be taken directly out of politics, or the hands of legislation, and given over to them. Dr. Chalmers saw the unspeakable absurdity of what we call our Almshouse system, and set himself to the replacing of it by agencies more genuine. Hospitals ought to follow the same law; and finally when every thing is ready, the Common School arrangement also.

All these, together with what may be done for the mitigation of war, and the correction of warlike sentiment, belong not to the state or to political management, but to the mercies and benignities, and faithful charities of private life, and particularly the private life of women. The state

is given to men ; these comprehend a vast circle
of powers and causes, almost equally extended,
that belong especially to women. We speak, for
example, of our Almshouse provisions—there
could not be a more naked lie ; for there is not
even a shred or semblance of alms in the case ; nothing but taxations to be gathered by law, and paid
over by legal officers. Not a feeling of mercy is
anywhere appealed to or felt. Our hospitals and
public schools are now getting to be more generally supported in the same way. Not a vestige
of benevolence is called into play ; the state is
managing now, not in a way to dispense, but
to dispense with benevolence! Our men are not
in it, because they are doing every thing politically, or by law. Our women can not be in it,
because it is taken away. And so we lose the
benefit of a whole best side of life. Here are
ministrations, teachings, offices, and magistracies
of mercy without number, all a great deal worthier
and higher than any that our women can hope to
obtain at the polls, but they do not see it. And
they are dying, they say, because they have
nothing to do!

Is it not time that, instead of going after these
political illusions, we begin to revise the great
prime falsity and imposture we have let into our
practice. I do not say that our present almshouse system, as we call it, is worse and more
cruel than nothing, but it is the most mischievous

and miserable thing we have borrowed from the mother country, most false in principle and worthiest to be stripped away. We have certain benefits from our common schools, but we are coming down rapidly now upon the fact, that no religion can be taught, and not even a religious morality, because it will infringe on some misbelief, or variant belief; and the charge that was laid by the Catholics is becoming more painfully just every year. Had our women every thing in train here, as they might and ought to have had, all these modes of beneficence would now be theirs, and they might even be complaining that their works are too heavy and too many.

Of course it will be seen, that when our Sisters of Charity, and others subject to the monastic garb and discipline, are going their rounds on errands of mercy, they, in fact, are acting under law as truly as they would be under the laws of the state, and are in exactly the same fault of principle we deplore in ourselves.

I can not exhaust this matter by any brief discussion, but it will be seen at a glance, how vast a field is open here to women. They will sometime have it,—I hope not a very long time hence,—and it will suffice to occupy their whole army.

But there is yet one thing more which must not be omitted, viz.: the great field opened for them by religion. The womanly nature, being a sub ject nature, is specially flexible and free to the Christian inspirations, and for this reason, doubtless, it is that more than twice as many women as men are engaged in Christian works and relations. Yet the call is now for women to buckle on the harness of political life and challenge the right to fight common battles with men. The subject nature is now to be adjourned, and the self-willed, governing nature to take its place; and the result will be, of course, that only half as many women will accept the cross, because they too are learning now to fight out their will; and the count of Christian men will also be reduced, because the number that have Christian wives who have grace to win their husbands is reduced. The result of course will be, if this reform is carried, that the number of them that believe will be greatly diminished, and whole centuries of toilsome progress will be lost, as it were, in a day. And yet the bitterest, heaviest part of the loss will fall upon the women who are expected to be the chief gainers in so great a change. In virtue of their subject nature, they now hold the Godward side of humanity, which is, in fact, the side of highest power; and abjuring their nature they, of course, abjure the power. Men will add their opinions to religion, even as rush-lights may be added to the sun; or sometimes they will flame on the world as prophets gifted with revelations that have no very exact keeping with the merit of their character, and are sometimes a prodigious miracle bursting up through manifold obliquities. Meantime women, far more religious in their habit, are never distinctly set in the prophetic office, though sometimes verbally honored in the prophetic title, for the reason simply, it would seem, that they are to be more than prophets, viz.: to obtain acquaintance with God in the higher plane of practical sainthood, and spiritual insight on the basis of experience. So they are to take their subject nature into the recesses of God's friendship, and have it there imbued with all understanding in the private mind of the Spirit, and are so to be known as knowing God. And there is no other character so divinely impressive, or so beautifully configured to God's purity; therefore none that is gifted with a power so transcendent.

Thus when Madame Guyon draws the great Fenelon to her confidence, and her cell in the prison; when she opens to him her conceptions of God's mysteries, and he, in faithful homage to her cause undertakes for her, and becomes her apologist, accepting her openly before her persecutors, what do we see in this impressive sight, but that learning and fame and genius, all widest influence and highest position, will come to pay their tribute to the woman who has found God's inspirations, and entered into the secret of his will. What Joan of Arc accomplished is scarcely a greater wonder. And thus again when that wonderful daughter of God, Madame Krudner, sought for and found by Alexander of Russia, kneels with him side by side, Protestant with Greek, night after night, endeavoring to guide him through his misgivings into the great future God will open for him and his allies, what do we see, in fact, but that she is holding sway, in simple sainthood, over all Europe, including the great Napoleon himself. These of course are extreme cases. But the womanly sainthood power is always doing this, in some way or manner less conspicuous. And the time is coming, if there is enough of subject nature left, when it will be crowned in the supreme queenhood of the world.

My object now in this brief, closing chapter, has been to show what fields of great endeavor and high public sway, what opportunities of advancement are even now and always set before the women of the nation. They are saying, and multitudes of men are conceding the fact on every hand, that they must get vent in political life or die for want of any thing to do. My fixed conviction is that no such thing is true. Their subject nature, which is called their subject condition, has here been shown, I think, to contain all the grandest possibilities of work and power and character that could or can be given them. It is in fact the prime endowment of their womanhood itself.

CHARLES SCRIBNER.   A. C. ARMSTRONG.   A. J. PEABODY.

Condensed Catalogue

OF THE PUBLICATIONS OF

CHARLES SCRIBNER & Co.,

654 BROADWAY,

NEW YORK.   JANUARY, 1868.

*** *The figures in the last column of this Catalogue refer to* CHARLES SCRIBNER & CO.'S *Descriptive Catalogue, copies of which will be sent to any address upon application.*

*** *Blanks in the column of prices, except in the case of School Text-Books, the prices of which may be learned from* CHARLES SCRIBNER & CO.'S *Educational Catalogue, indicate that the Works are either out of print or in press.*

*** *In this list the names of Books just published are given in* SMALL CAPITALS; *those issued during the year 1867, as well as new editions of Works previously produced, are indicated by italics.*

*** *The prices here given are for the regular style of binding in cloth. Books furnished in other styles, and their respective prices, may be learned from the Descriptive Catalogue.*

*** *Any of these Books will be sent post-paid to any address upon receipt of the price.*

	Volumes.	Size.	Price.	Page
ADAMS, W., D.D.				
THANKSGIVING	1	12mo	$2 00	2
Three Gardens	1	12mo	2 00	1
AGASSIZ, PROF. LOUIS.				
Structure of Animal Life (The)	1	8vo	2 50	2
ALEXANDER, A., D.D.				
Moral Science	1	12mo	1 50	3
ALEXANDER, J. W., D.D.				
Alexander, Archibald, Life of, (Portrait)	1	12mo	2 00	3
Christian Faith and Practice (Discourses)	1	12mo	2 00	6
Consolation (Discourses)	1	12mo	2 00	5
Faith (Discourses)	1	12mo	2 00	6
Forty Years' Correspondence with a Friend	2	12mo	4 00	4
Preaching, Thoughts on	1	12mo	2 00	5

Charles Scribner & Co.'s Condensed Catalogue.

	Volumes.	Size.	Price.	Page.
ALEXANDER, J. A., D.D.				
Acts (Commentary)	2	12mo	$4 00	8
Isaiah " (complete)	2	8vo	6 50	7
" " (abridged)	2	12mo	4 00	8
Mark "	1	12mo	2 00	8
Matthew "	1	12mo	2 00	8
Psalms "	3	12mo	6 00	7
New Test. Literature and Ecc. Hist.	1	12mo	2 00	9
Sermons (with Portrait)	2	12mo	———	9
ALLSTON, WASHINGTON.				
Lectures and Poems	1	12mo	2 50	9
ANDREWS, REV. S. J.				
Life of Our Lord	1	post 8vo	3 00	10
ARMSTRONG, G. D., D.D.				
Works of	3	12mo ea.	1 25	11
BAUTAIN, PROF. A.				
Extempore Speaking	1	12mo	1 50	12
BEECHER, REV. H. W.				
Prayers from Plymouth Pulpit	1	12mo	1 75	13
BOTTA, PROF.				
Dante as Poet, Patriot, Philosopher	1	crown 8vo	2 50	14
BRACE, CHARLES L.				
Hungary, with Experience of Austrian Police,	1	12mo	———	15
Home Life in Germany	1	12mo	———	14
Norse Folk	1	12mo	2 00	15
Races of Old World	1	post 8vo	2 50	15
Short Sermons for Newsboys	1	16mo	1 50	16
BUSHNELL, HORACE, D.D.				
Character of Jesus	1	18mo	1 00	19
Christ and his Salvation	1	12mo	2 00	19
Christian Nurture	1	12mo	2 00	18
Nature and the Supernatural	1	12mo	2 25	17
New Life, Sermons for	1	12mo	2 00	19
Vicarious Sacrifice, The	1	8vo	3 00	18
Work and Play	1	12mo	2 00	19
CHEEVER, G. B., D.D.				
Works of	3	12mo	———	20
CLARK, PROF. N. G.				
English Language, Elements of	1	12mo	1 25	21
COLLIER, J. PAYNE, F.S.A.				
Rarest Books in English Language	4	small 8vo	12 00	21
CONYBEARE, REV. W. J., and HOWSON, REV. J. S.				
St. Paul, Life and Epistles of (illustrated)	2	8vo	7 50	22

	Volumes.	Size.	Price.	Page.
COOK, PROF. J. P., JR.				
Religion and Chemistry	1	crown 8vo	$2 50	24
CRAIK, GEO. L., LL.D.				
English Literature and Language	2	8vo	7 50	23
CROSBY, PROF. HOWARD, D.D.				
New Testament with Notes	1	12mo	1 50	24
CRUMMELL, REV. A.				
Africa, Future of	1	12mo	1 00	—
DANA, A. H.				
Ethical and Physiological Inquiries	1	12mo	1 50	25
DANA, R. H.				
Poems and Prose Writings	2	12mo	4 00	25
DAWSON, HENRY B.				
Fœderalist (Univ. Ed.)	1	8vo	3 00	25
" with Notes	1	8vo	3 75	25
DAY, PROF. H. N.				
ENGLISH COMPOSITION	1	12mo	1 50	26
DISCOURSE, (Rhetoric)	1	12mo	1 50	26
Logic	1	12mo	1 50	27
DERBY, EDWARD, EARL OF.				
Homer's Iliad (translated)	2	crown 8vo	5 00	28
DE VERE, M. SCHELE, LL.D.				
Studies in English	1	crown 8vo	2 50	29
DINGMAN, J. H.				
Publisher's Sheet-Book	1	Folio	15 00	29
DRUMMOND, REV. JAS.				
Christian Life, Thoughts for	1	12mo	1 50	30
DUYCKINCK, E. A. and G. L.				
Cyclopædia of Am. Literature (400 Portraits, &c.)	2	royal 8vo	10 00	31
DWIGHT, BENJ. W.				
Philology, Modern	2	8vo	6 00	30
ELLET, MRS. E. F.				
American Revolution, Domestic History of	1	12mo	1 50	32
" " Women of	3	12mo	—	33
Pioneer Women of the West	1	12mo	1 50	32
QUEENS OF AM. SOCIETY (13 steel engravings)	1	12mo	2 50	33
ELLIOTT, CHARLES W.				
New England History	2	8vo	6 00	34
EWBANK, THOS.				
Hydraulics	1	8vo	6 00	34
FELTER, S. A.				
Arithmetics, Natural Series of	1	—	—	35–36

	Volumes.	Size.	Price.	Page
FIELD, HENRY M., D.D.				
Atlantic Telegraph, History of	1	12mo	$1 75	37
FISHER, REV. PROF. GEO. P.				
Supernatural Origin of Christianity	1	8vo	2 50	38
Silliman, Benj., LL.D., Life of (Portrait)	2	crown 8vo	5 00	37
FORSYTH, WM.				
Cicero, New Life of (Illustrations)	2	crown 8vo	5 00	39
FOWLER W. C., LL.D.				
Sectional Controversy (The)	1	8vo	1 75	39
FROUDE, J. A.				
HISTORY OF ENGLAND	10	crown 8vo	3 00 ea.	40
SHORT STUDIES ON GREAT SUBJECTS	1	crown 8vo	3 00	41
GAGE, REV. W. L.				
Carl Ritter, Life of	1	12mo	2 00	42
GASPARIN, COUNT.				
America before Europe	1	12mo	2 00	42
GIBBONS, J. S.				
PUBLIC DEBT OF THE UNITED STATES	1	crown 8vo	2 00	43
GUIZOT, M.				
Meditations (First and Second Series)	2	12mo ea.	1 75	43
GUYOT, PROF. ARNOLD.				
Geographies, Wall Maps, Key, etc.	—	—	—	44-47
HALL, EDWIN, D.D.				
Puritans and their Principles	1	8vo	2 50	48
HALSEY, REV. LEROY J.				
Bible, Literary Attractions of	1	12mo	1 75	48
HEADLEY, J. T.				
Complete Works of	15			49, 53
HEIDELBERG,				
Catechism	1	small 4to	3 50	54
HERBERT, H. W.				
Works of	3	12mo ea.	1 50	54
HOLLAND, DR. J. G. (Timothy Titcomb.)				
Bay-Path. A Novel	1	12mo	2 00	58
Bitter-Sweet. A Poem	1	12mo	1 50	56
Gold Foil	1	12mo	1 75	56
Kathrina. A Poem	1	12mo	1 50	59
Lessons in Life	1	12mo	1 75	57
Letters to the Joneses	1	12mo	1 75	57
Letters to Young People	1	12mo	1 50	55
Miss Gilbert's Career	1	12mo	2 00	59
Plain Talks on Familiar Subjects	1	12mo	1 75	58

	Volumes.	Size.	Price.	Page.
HOURS AT HOME.				
A FAMILY MAGAZINE		Per annum	$3 00	6c
HURST, REV. J. F.				
Rationalism, History of	1	8vo	3 50	61
JAMESON, JUDGE J. A.				
Constitutional Convention	1	8vo	4 50	62
JOHNSON, ANNA C. (MINNIE MYRTLE).				
Cottages of the Alps	1	12mo	——	63
Germany, Peasant Life in	1	12mo	——	63
Myrtle Wreath	1	12mo	1 25	63
JONES, CHARLES COLCOCK, D.D.				
HISTORY OF THE CHURCH OF GOD	2	8vo ea.	3 50	63
KIRKLAND, MRS. C. M.				
Evening Book	1	12mo	1 25	65
Holidays Abroad	2	12mo	2 00	65
Patriotic Eloquence	1	12mo	1 75	64
School Garland	1	12mo	——	64
KNOX, REV. J. B.				
St. Thomas, W. I., History of	1	12mo	$1 25	65
LABOULAYE EDOUARD.				
Paris in America	1	12mo	1 25	69
LANGE, PROF. J. P., D.D.				
Commentary on Scriptures, Theolog. and Homiletical: Matthew (1); MARK AND LUKE (1); ACTS (1); JAMES, PETER, JOHN, JUDE (1); CORINTHIANS (1); THESSALONIANS, TIMOTHY, TITUS, PHILEMON, HEBREWS (1); GENESIS, (1)		8vo ea.	5 00	66–68
LAWRENCE, EUGENE.				
British Historians, Lives of	2	12mo	3 50	69
LIBER LIBRORUM	1	16mo	1 50	70
LORD, JOHN, LL.D.				
OLD ROMAN WORLD	1	crown 8vo	3 00	70
LYNCH, LIEUT. W. F.				
Naval Life	1	12mo	1 50	71
McLEOD, ALEX., D.D.				
Life of, by Rev. S. B. Wylie	1	8vo	2 00	114
MACDONALD, J. M., D.D.				
My Father's House	1	12mo	1 50	72
MACLEOD, DONALD,				
Works of	3	12mo ea.	1 25	71
MAGOON, REV. E. L.				
Living Orators in America	1	12mo	1 75	72
Orators of the American Revolution	1	12mo		72

	Volumes.	Size.	Price.	Page

MAINE, HENRY S.
Ancient Law . . . . 1 crown 8vo $3 00   73

MARSH, HON. GEO. P.
English Language, Lectures on . . . 1 crown 8vo 3 00   74
"   "   Origin and History of . 1 crown 8vo 3 00   74
Man and Nature . . . . 1 crown 8vo 3 00   75

MARSH, J., D.D.
Temperance Recollections 1   12mo   2 25   76

MASON, J. M., D.D.
Complete Works . . . . 4 post 8vo ——   76

MEARS, REV. J. W.
Bible and the Workshop 1   12mo   1 00   76

MITCHELL, DONALD G. (IK MARVEL).
Dream Life 1   12mo $1 75   77
Dr. Johns: A Novel 2   12mo   3 50   79
Fresh Gleanings 1   12mo   ——   78
Lorgnette, The 1   12mo   ——   78
My Farm of Edgewood 1   12mo   1 75   79
Reveries of a Bachelor 1   12mo   1 75   77
Rural Studies 1   12mo   1 75   80
Seven Stories 1   12mo   1 75   78
Wet Days at Edgewood 1   12mo   1 75   80

MITCHEL, PROF. O. M.
Astronomy of the Bible 1   12mo   1 75   81
Planetary and Stellar Worlds . . . 1   12mo   1 75   81
Popular Astronomy 1   12mo   1 75   81

MORRIS, GEO. P.
Poetical Works (blue and gold) . . 1   16mo   1 50   83

MULLER MAX.
Science of Language, Lectures on . . 1 crown 8vo 2 50   82
"   "   "   (Second Series)   3 50   82

NEWCOMB, REV. H.
Missions, Cyclopædia of (32 Maps) . . 1   8vo   ——   83

ORLEANS, DUCHESS OF.
Memoirs of (Portrait) 1   12mo   86

OWEN, J. J., D.D.
Commentaries on the New Testament: *Matthew* (1); MARK AND LUKE (1); JOHN (1); ACTS (—), in press; GENESIS (—), in press   1   12mo ea. 1 75   84–85

PAEZ, DON RAMON.
South America, Wild Scenes in . . . 1 crown 8vo 2 50   86

PAULDING, JAMES K.
Literary Life of (1); BULLS AND JONATHANS (1); TALES OF THE GOOD WOMAN (1); A BOOK OF VAGARIES (1); DUTCHMAN'S FIRESIDE . . . . each 1 crown 8vo 2 50   87

	Volumes.	Size.	Price.	Page.
PERCE, ELBERT.				
Magnetic Globes			—	88
PERRY, PROF. A. L.				
Political Economy, Elements of . . .	1	crown 8vo	2 50	89
PRENTISS, S. S.				
Life of, by Geo. L. Prentiss, D.D. . .	2	12mo	3 50	86
PRIME, S. I., D.D.				
Power of Prayer	1	12mo	1 50	90
PUBLIC PRAYER.				
Book of	1	12mo	2 00	13
RANDOLPH, A. D. F.				
Hopefully Waiting, and other Verses . .	1	16mo	$1 50	90.
SCHAFF, P., D.D.				
Apostolic Church, History of . . .	1	8vo	3 75	91
CHRISTIAN " - " . . .	3	8vo ea.	3 75	92–93
PERSON OF CHRIST . . .	1	16mo	1 50	94
SEAMAN, E. C.				
Progress of Nations	1	12mo		94
SHEDD, W. G. T., D.D.				
Christian Doctrine, History of . . .	2	8vo	6 50	95
HOMILETICS AND PASTORAL THEOLOGY .	1	8vo	3 50	96
SHELDON, E. A.				
Model Lessons on Objects, etc. . . .				97
SILLIMAN, BEN. M.D.				
Life of, by Professor Geo. P. Fisher . .	2	crown 8vo	5 00	37
SIMMS, W. G.				
Huguenots in Florida	1	12mo	1 50	—
SMITH, PROF. H. B., D.D.				
Christian Church, History of, in Tabular Form	1	Folio	6 75	98–99
SMITH, J. H.				
Gilead ; or, The Vision of All Souls' Hospital	1	12mo	1 50	100
SMITH, MRS. MARY HOWE.				
Lessons on the Globe	1	12mo	0 50	88
SPRING, GARDINER, D.D.				
Personal Reminiscences, etc. (Portrait)	2	12mo	4 00	100
STANLEY, DEAN A. P.				
Eastern Church	1	8vo	4 00	101
Jewish Church, Lectures on (First Series) .	1	8vo	4 00	101
" " " (Second Series)	1	8vo	5 00	{ 101 / 102 }
Sermons	1	12mo	1 50	103
STRICKLAND, AGNES.				
QUEENS OF ENGLAND, LIVES OF . . .	1	12mo	2 00	103

	Volumes.	Size.	Price.	Page
TAYLOR, GEORGE.				
Indications of the Creator.	1	12mo	1 75	105
TENNEY, S., A.M.				
Natural History	1	crown 8vo	3 00	104
" " Library Edition	1	large 8vo	4 00	104
" " for Schools	1	12mo	2 00	104
TIMOTHY TITCOMB.				
Complete Works of. See HOLLAND.	—	—	—	55–59
TRENCH, RT. REV. R. C.				
Epistles to Seven Churches, Commentary on	1	12mo	1 50	106
Studies in the Gospels	1	8vo	3 00	106
Glossary of English Words	1	12mo	1 50	107
Synonyms of New Testament (1st and 2d Series)	2	12mo ea.	1 25	107
TUCKERMAN, H. T.				
America and her Commentators	1	crown 8vo	2 50	108
TULLIDGE, REV. H.				
Triumphs of the Bible	1	12mo	2 00	108
TUTHILL, MRS. L. C.				
Joy and Care. Book for Young Mothers	1	16mo	1 00	109
VAN SANTVOORD, GEO.				
Lives of Chief Justices of U. S.	1	8vo		109
WHITNEY, PROF. W. D.				
LANGUAGE, AND THE STUDY OF LANGUAGE	1	crown 8vo	2 50	110
WILLIS, N. P.				
Complete Works of				111 / 112
WISE, CAPT. H. A.				
Works of	2	12mo ea.	1 75	112
WOOLSEY, PREST. T. D.				
International Law, Introduction to	1	8vo	2 50	113
WYLIE, S. B., D.D.				
McLeod, Alexander, Life of	1	8vo	2 00	114
ZINCKE, F. BARHAM.				
Extempory Preaching	1	12mo	1 50	114

ILLUSTRATED GIFT-BOOKS.

‎‎* *In this list the prices of the respective works as bound in cloth, full gilt, are given. All of them, however, are furnished in Turkey morocco, and the prices of these editions may be learned by reference to the catalogue.*

	Price.	Page.		Price	Page
ÆSOP'S FABLES	$18 00	117	FRED AND MARIA AND ME	$1 50	121
Bitter-Sweet	9 00	117	Folk Songs	15 00	115
Book of Rubies	7 00	119	MY FARM OF EDGEWOOD	10 00	121
Christian Armor	15 00	120	Pilgrim's Progress	5 00	120
Cotter's Saturday Night	5 00	119	QUEENS OF AMERICAN SOCIETY	6 00	118
FLORAL BELLES	25 00	116			

www.ingramcontent.com/pod-product-compliance
Lightning Source LLC
Chambersburg PA
CBHW030735250426
43671CB00035B/435